the music glee

season two   volume 4

Series Artwork, Fox Trademarks and Logos
TM and © 2011 Twentieth Century Fox Film Corporation.
All Rights Reserved.

ISBN 978-1-4584-0695-8

HAL•LEONARD®
CORPORATION
7777 W. BLUEMOUND RD. P.O. BOX 13819 MILWAUKEE, WI 53213

Visit Hal Leonard Online at
www.halleonard.com

EMPIRE STATE OF MIND

Words and Music by ALICIA KEYS,
SHAWN CARTER, JANE'T SEWELL,
ANGELA HUNTE, AL SHUCKBURGH,
BERT KEYES and SYLVIA ROBINSON

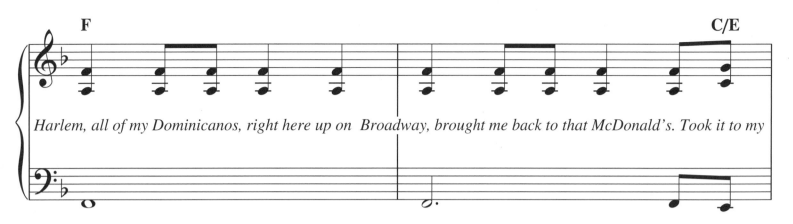

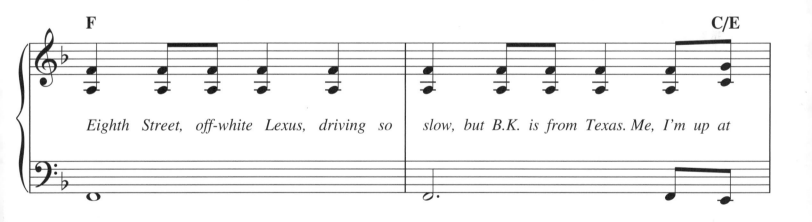

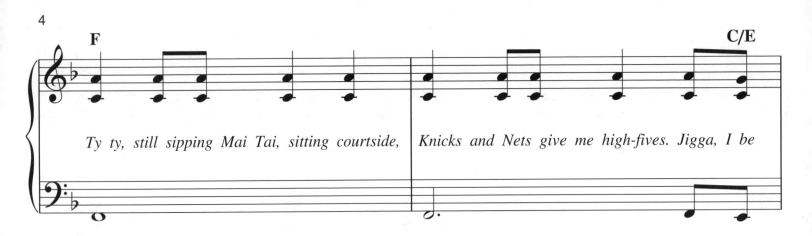

Ty ty, still sipping Mai Tai, sitting courtside, Knicks and Nets give me high-fives. Jigga, I be

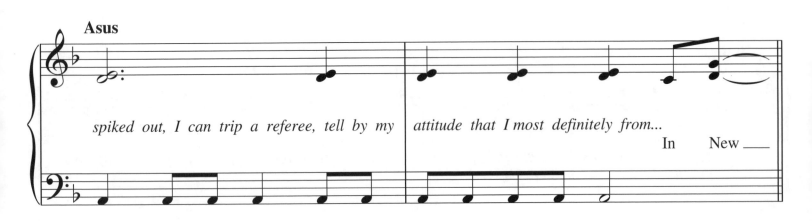

spiked out, I can trip a referee, tell by my attitude that I most definitely from... In New

York concrete jungle where dreams are made of, there's noth-ing you can't

do. Now you're in New York, these streets will make you feel brand-

Additional Lyrics

2. Catch me at the X with OG at a Yankee game
   Dude, I made the Yankee hat more famous than a Yankee can.
   You should know I bleed blue, but I ain't a crip though,
   But I got a gang of brothas walking with my clique though.

   Welcome to the melting pot, corners where we're selling rocks,
   Afrika bambaataa, home of the hip-hop,
   Yellowcab, Gypsy cab, dollar cab, holla back,
   For Foreigners it ain't for they act like they forgot how to act.

   Eight million stories out there and they're naked.
   City, it's a pity half of y'all won't make it.
   Me, I gotta plug Special Ed, I got it made,
   If Jeezy's paying LeBron, I'm paying Dwayne Wade.

   3 dice, Cee Lo, 3-Card Monte,
   Labor Day parade, rest in peace Bob Marley.
   Statue of Liberty, long live the World Trade,
   Long live the King, yo, I'm from the Empire State that's...

3. Lights is blinding, girls need blinders
   So they can step out of bounds quick.
   The sidelines is blind with casualties, who sip your life casually,
   Then gradually become worse. Don't bite the apple, Eve.

   Caught up in the in-crowd, now you're in style,
   And in the winter gets cold, en vogue with your skin out,
   The city of sin is a pity on a whim,
   Good girls gone bad, the city's filled with them.

   Mami took a bus trip, now she got her bust out,
   Everybody ride her, just like a bus route.
   Hail Mary to the city, you're a virgin,
   And Jesus can't save you, life starts when the church in.

   Came here for school, graduated to the high life.
   Ball players, rap stars, addicted to the limelight.
   MD, MA got you feeling like a champion,
   The city never sleeps, better slip you an Ambien.

BILLIONAIRE

Words and Music by TRAVIS McCOY,
PHILIP LAWRENCE, BRUNO MARS
and ARI LEVINE

Moderate Reggae feel

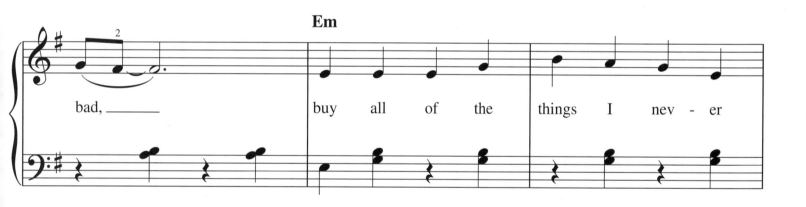

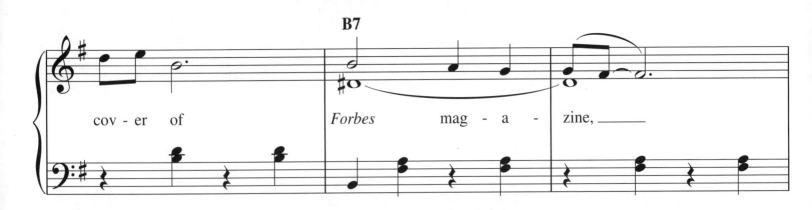

cov - er of   *Forbes*   mag - a - zine, _____

smil - in' next to   O - prah and the   Queen. _____

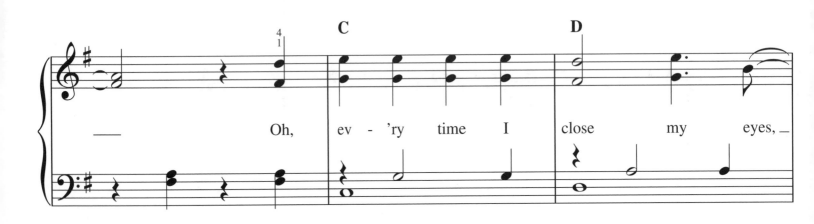

_____   Oh,   ev - 'ry   time   I   close   my   eyes, _

_____   I   see   my   name   in

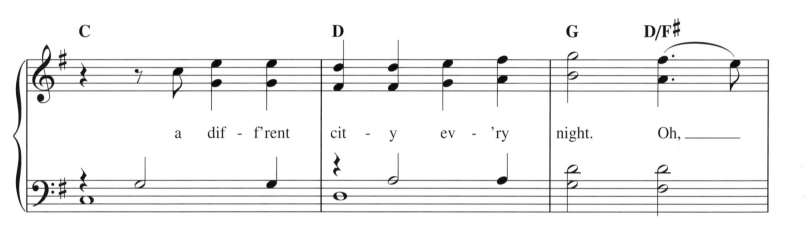

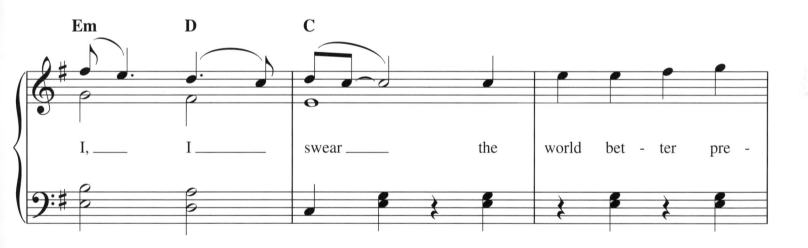

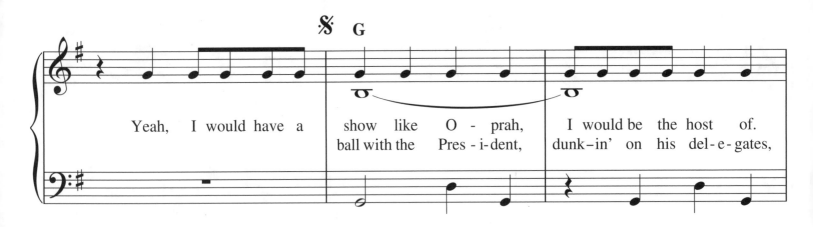

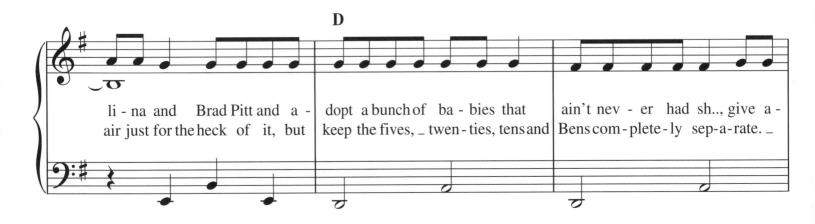

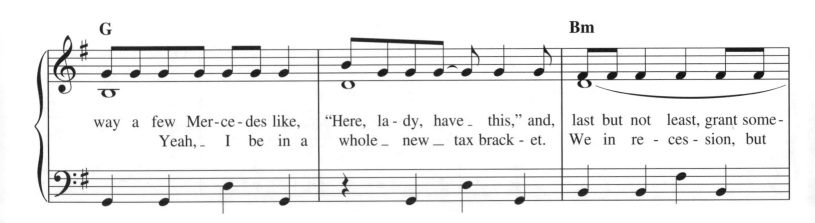

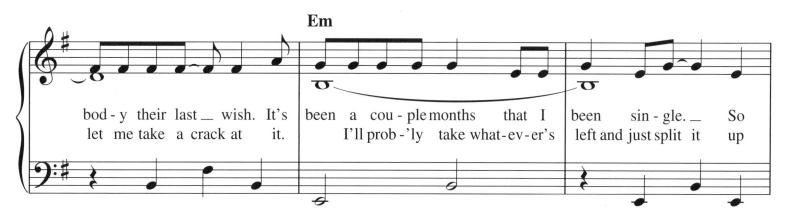

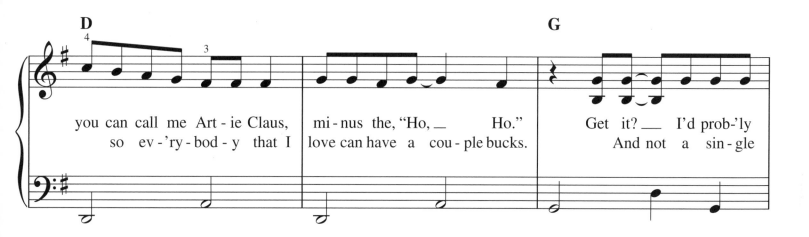

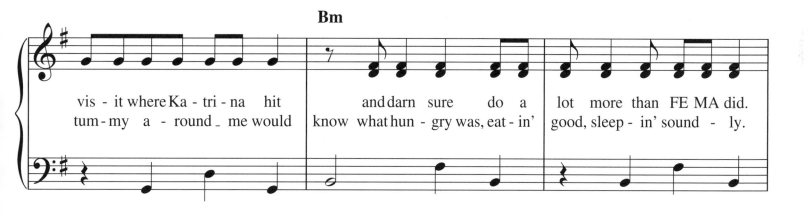

To Coda ⊕

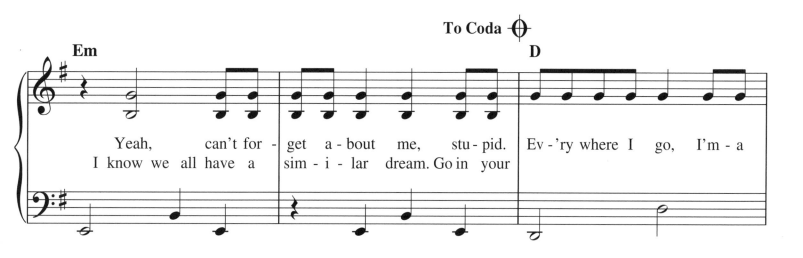

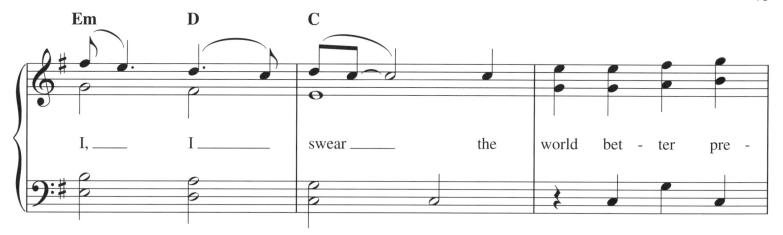

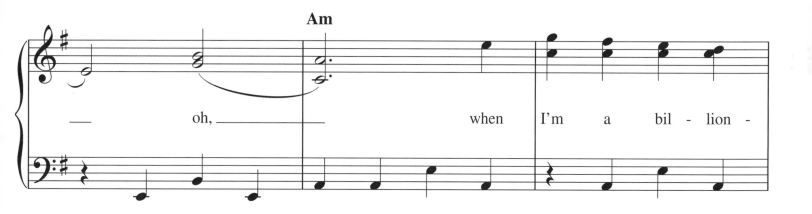

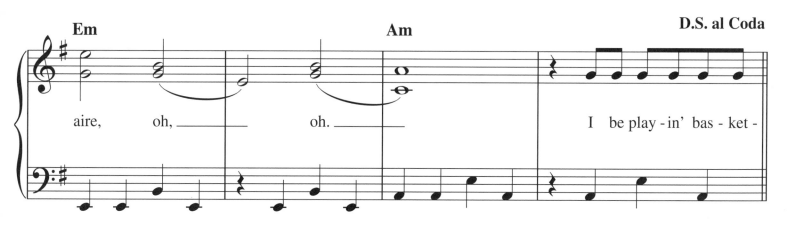

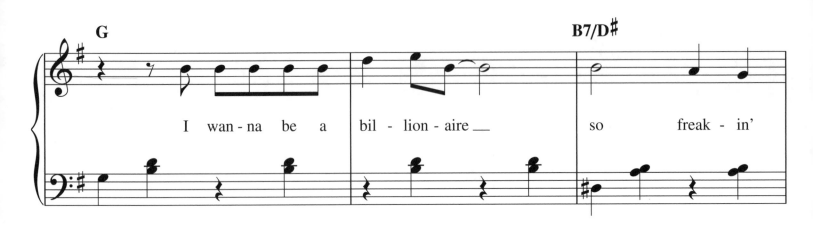

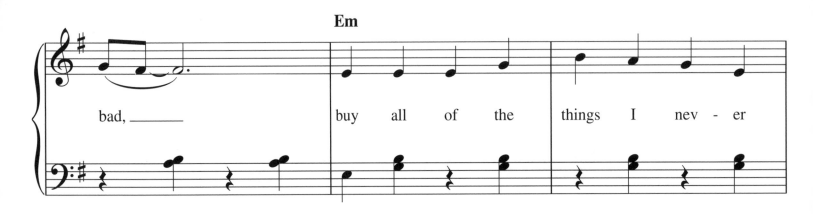

cov - er of   *Forbes*   mag - a - zine, _____

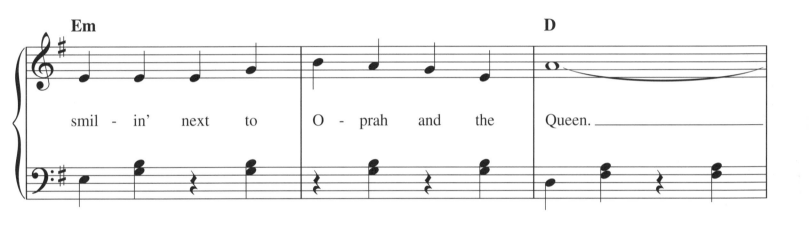

smil - in' next to   O - prah and the   Queen. _____

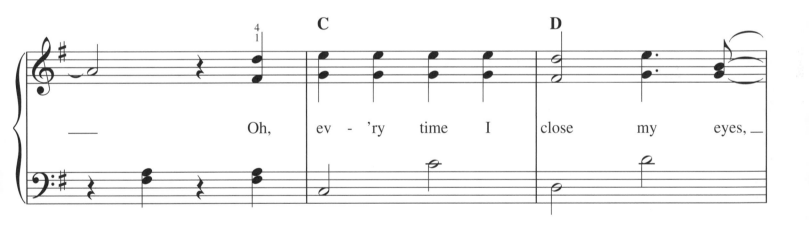

_____   Oh,   ev - 'ry time I   close my   eyes, __

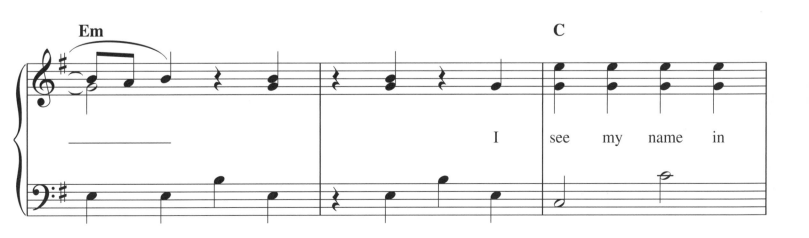

_____   I   see my name in

shin - ing lights. _____ Yeah, _____

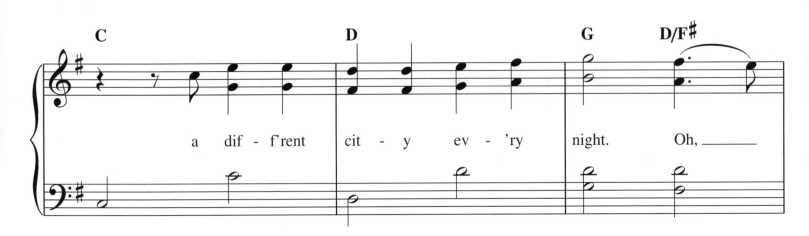

a dif - f'rent cit - y ev - 'ry night. Oh, _____

I, ____ I _____ swear _____ the world bet - ter pre -

pare _____ for when I'm a bil - lion - aire, oh, _____

ME AGAINST THE MUSIC

Words and Music by TERIUS NASH, CHRISTOPHER STEWART,
DORIAN HARDNETT, GARY O'BRIEN, BRITNEY SPEARS,
THABISO NKHEREANYE and MADONNA CICCONE

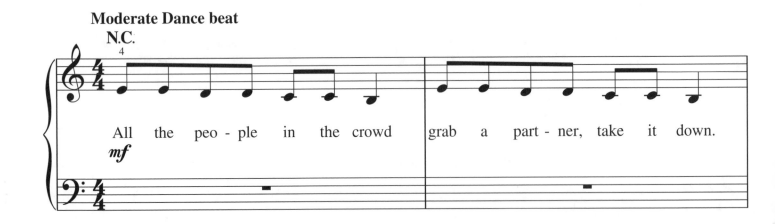

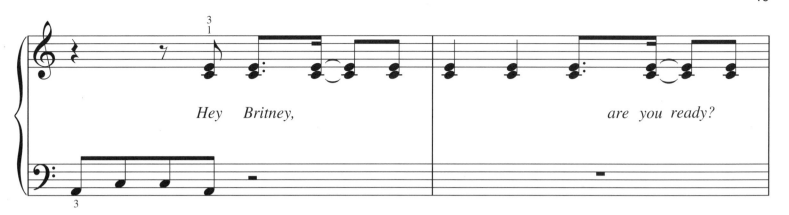

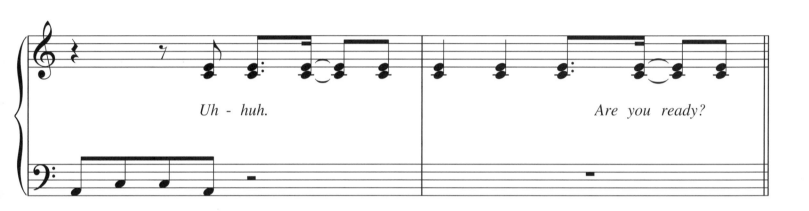

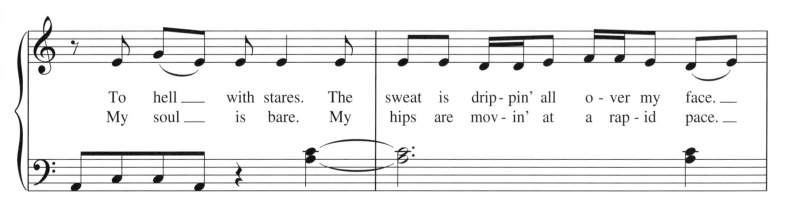

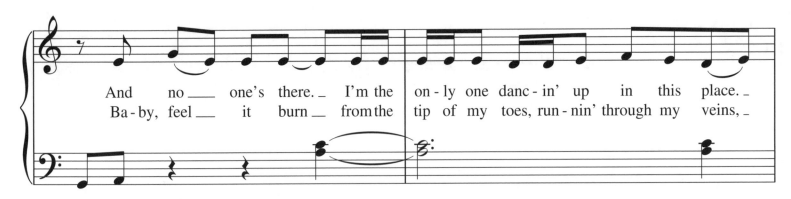

And no ___ one's there. ___ I'm the | on-ly one danc-in' up in this place. ___
Ba-by, feel ___ it burn ___ from the | tip of my toes, run-nin' through my veins, ___

To-night ___ I'm here. ___ Feel the | beat of the drum, got-ta get with that bass. }
and now's ___ your turn. ___ Let me | see what you got, don't ___ hes - i - tate. } I'm

up a-gainst the speak-er try'n' to take on the mu-sic. It's like a

com-pe-ti-tion, me a-gainst the beat. I wan-na get in the

zone. _____ I wan-na get in the zone. _____ If you

real - ly wan - na bat - tle, sad - dle up and get your rhy - thm. Try'n' to

hit it, chic - a - ta. In a min - ute, I'm a take a you

on. _____ I'm a take a you on, ____ hey, hey, hey.

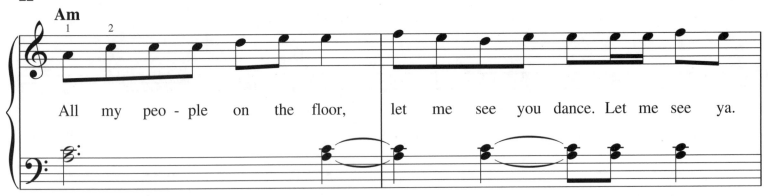

All my peo - ple on the floor, let me see you dance. Let me see ya.

All my peo - ple want - in' more, let me see you dance. I wan - na see ya.

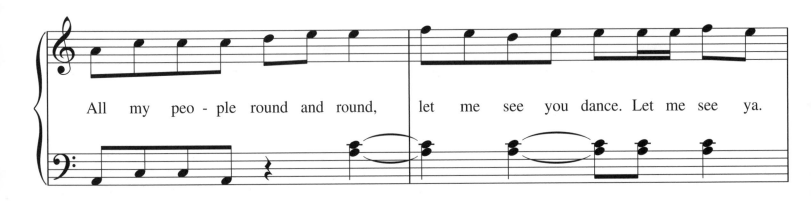

All my peo - ple round and round, let me see you dance. Let me see ya.

All my peo - ple in the crowd, let me see you dance. I wan - na see ya.

How would you like a friend-ly com - pe - ti - tion? Let's take on the

song. _____ Let's take on your song. __ It's

you and me, ba - by, we're the mu - sic. Time to par - ty all night

long. All night long. __

24

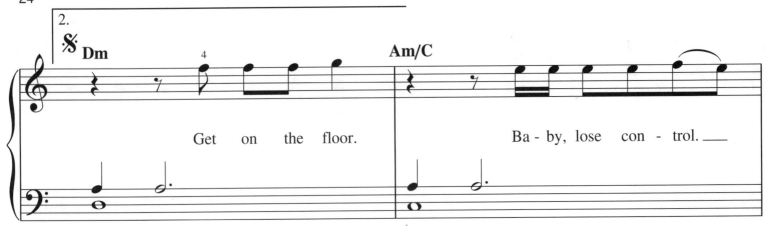

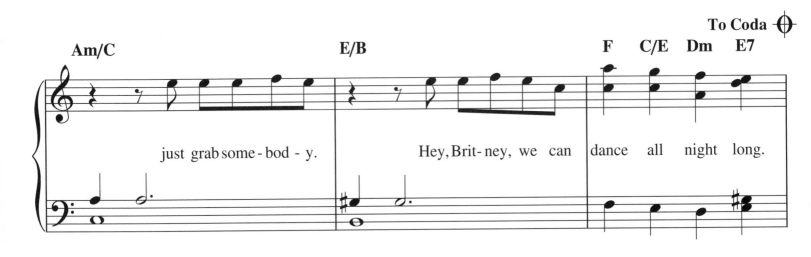

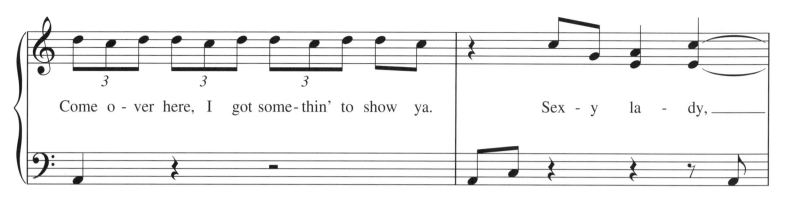

Come o - ver here, I got some-thin' to show ya. Sex - y la - dy, ___

___ I'd rath - er see you bare ___ your soul. If you

think you're so hot, bet - ter show me what you got. All my peo - ple in the crowd,

let me see you dance. Come on, Brit ney, lose con - trol. Grab a part - ner take it down.

CODA

All my peo - ple on the floor, let me see you dance. Let me see ya.

All my peo - ple want - in' more, let me see you dance. I wan - na see ya.

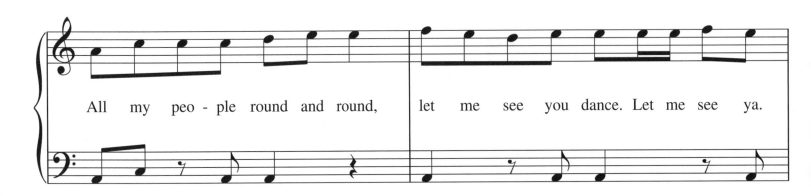

All my peo - ple round and round, let me see you dance. Let me see ya.

All my peo - ple in the crowd, let me see you dance. I wan - na see ya.

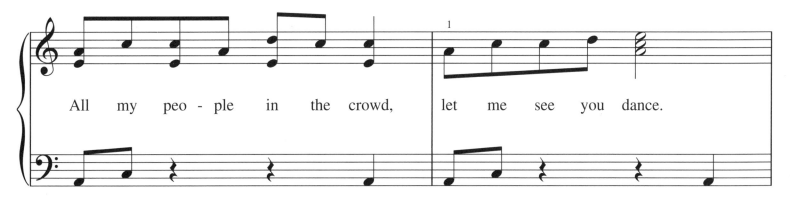

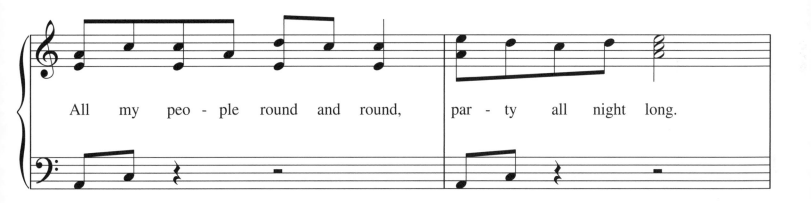

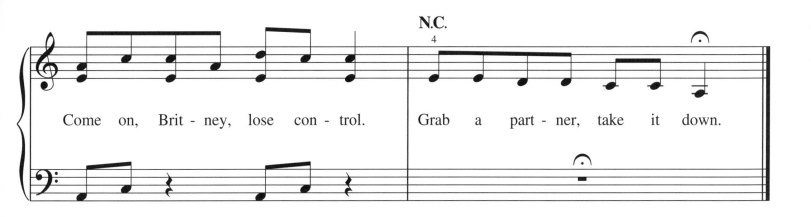

STRONGER

Words and Music by MARTIN SANDBERG
and RAMI YACOUB

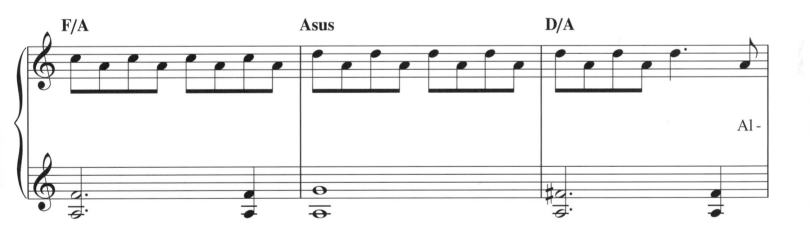

TOXIC

Words and Music by CATHY DENNIS,
CHRISTIAN KARLSSON, PONTUS WINNBERG
and HENRIK JONBACK

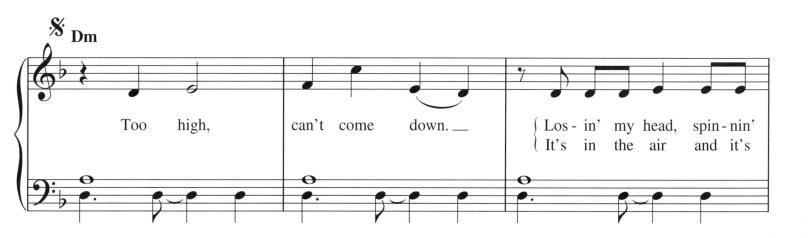

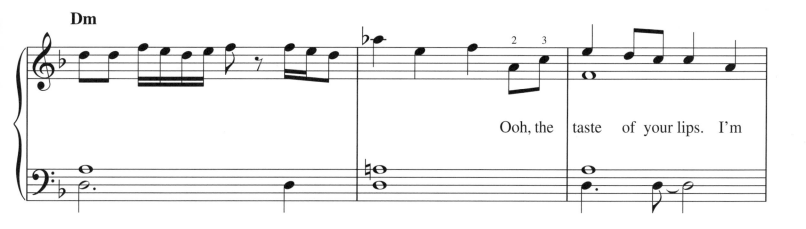

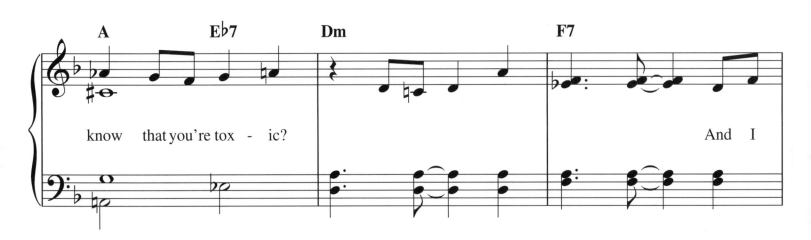

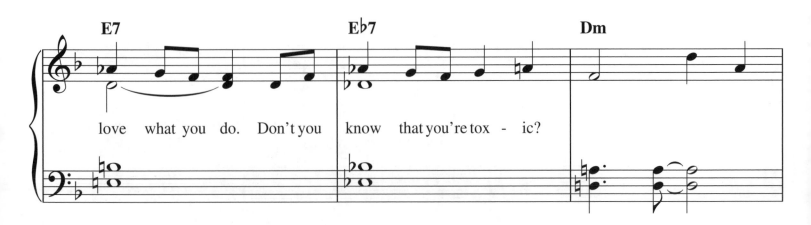

It's get-tin' late   to give you up.   I took a sip

from a dev-il's cup.   Slow - ly,   it's tak-ing o - ver me.

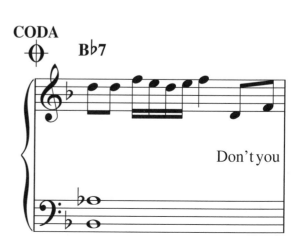

Don't you

THE ONLY EXCEPTION

Words and Music by HAYLEY WILLIAMS
and JOSH FARRO

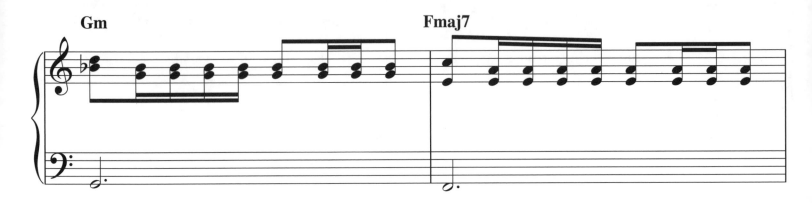

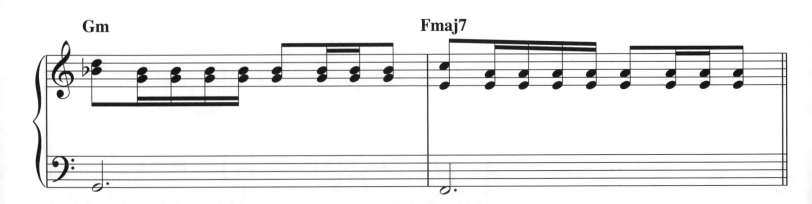

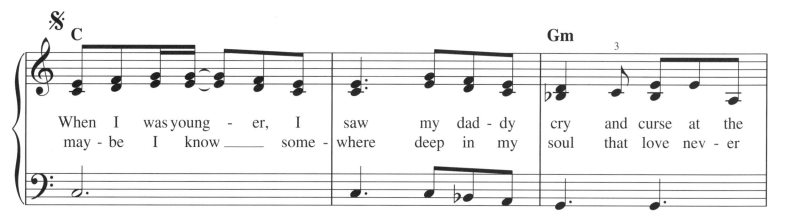

When I was young - er, I saw my dad - dy cry and curse at the
may - be I know _____ some - where deep in my soul that love nev - er

wind. _____ He broke his own heart, and I watched as he tried to
lasts. _____ And we've got to find oth - er ways to make it a -

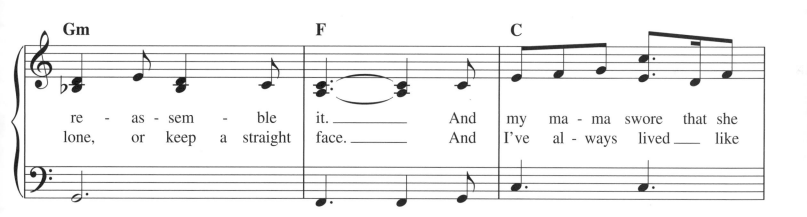

re - as - sem - ble it. _____ And my ma - ma swore that she
lone, or keep a straight face. _____ And I've al - ways lived ___ like

would nev - er let her - self for - get. _____ And
this, keep - ing a com - f'ta - ble dis - tance. _____ And

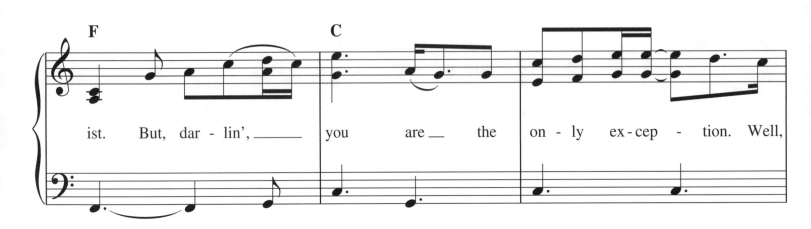

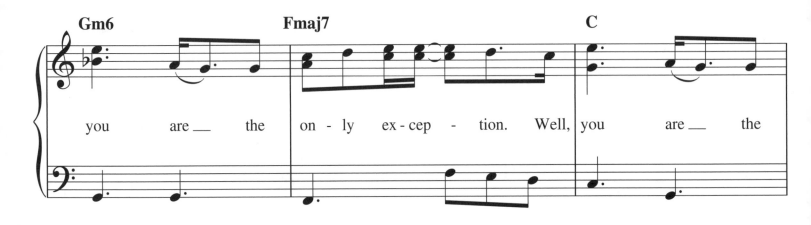

D.S. al Coda

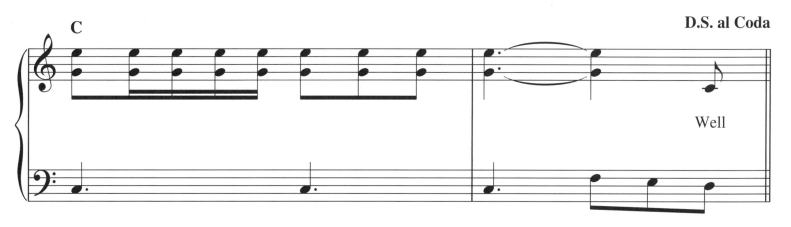

Well

ness, be - cause none of it was ev - er worth the risk. Well,

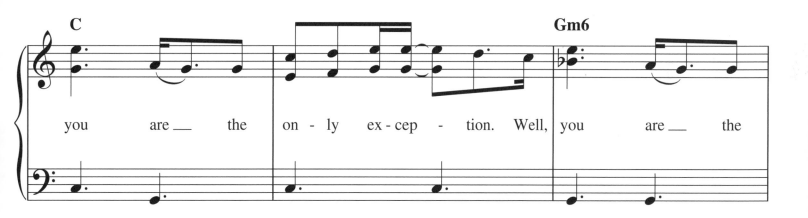

you are ___ the on - ly ex - cep - tion. Well, you are ___ the

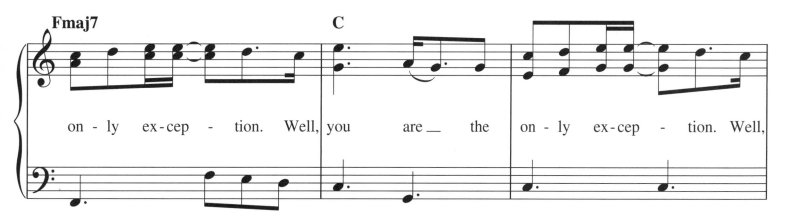

on - ly ex - cep - tion. Well, you are ___ the on - ly ex - cep - tion. Well,

you are the on - ly ex - cep - tion. __

I've got a tight grip on re - al - i - ty, but I can't __ let

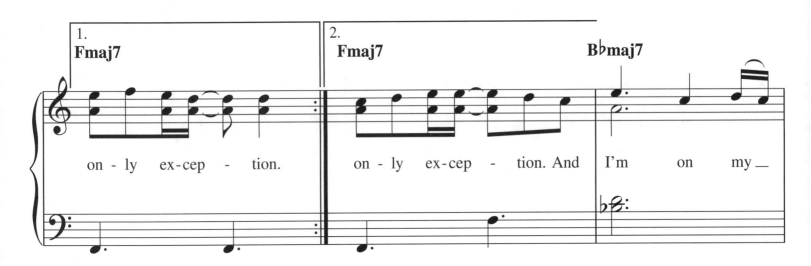

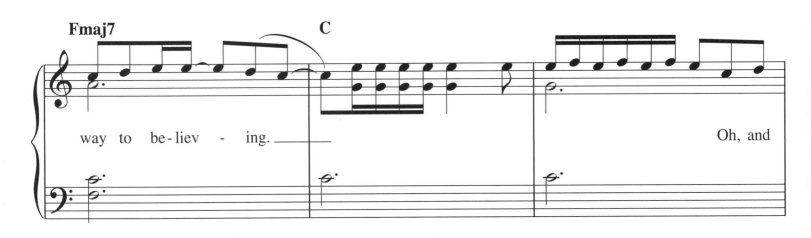

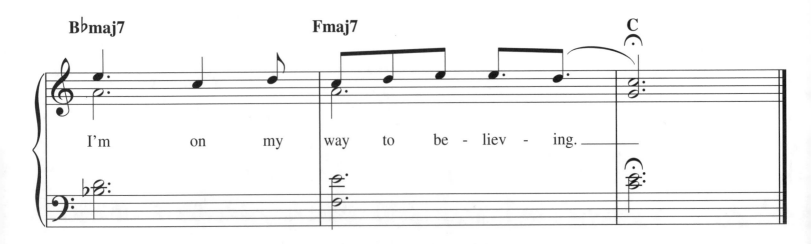

I WANT TO HOLD YOUR HAND

Words and Music by JOHN LENNON
and PAUL McCARTNEY

With a steady Rock beat

Oh yeah,
I'll _____ tell you some - thing
please ____ say to me _____

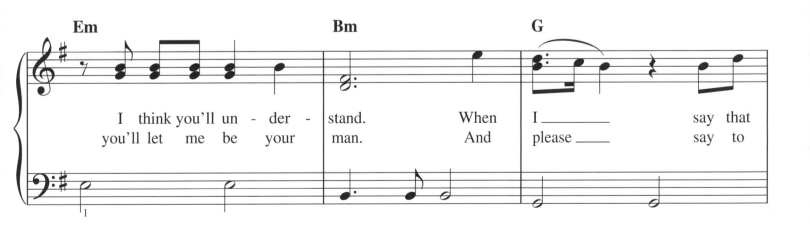

I think you'll un - der - stand.
you'll let me be your man.

When
And
I _____ say that
please ____ say to

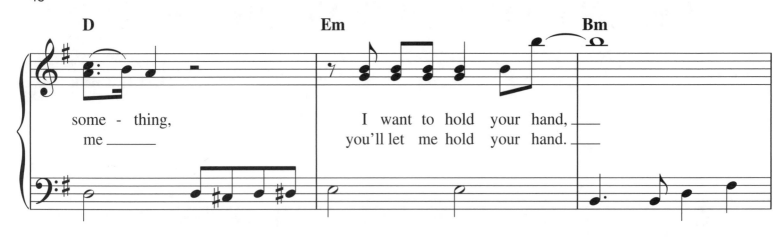

some - thing,
me _____

I want to hold your hand,
you'll let me hold your hand.

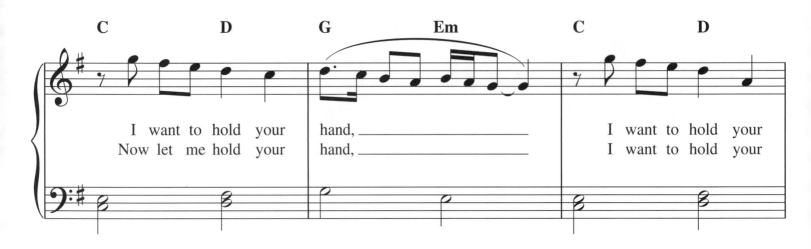

I want to hold your
Now let me hold your

hand, _____

I want to hold your
I want to hold your

1.

hand.   Oh, ___

2.

hand.

And when I

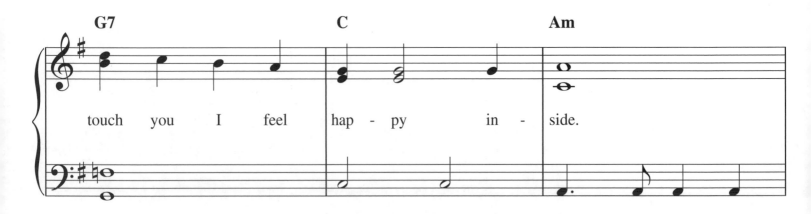

touch   you I feel   hap - py   in - side.

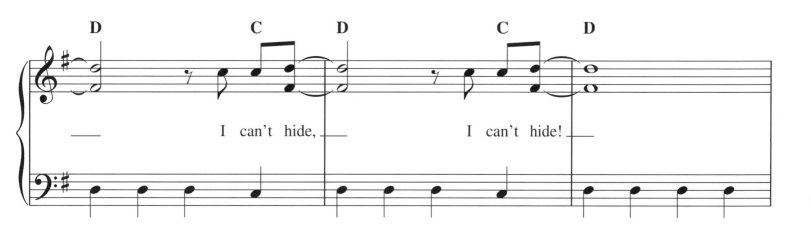

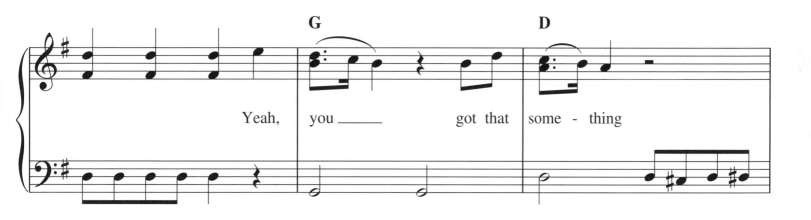

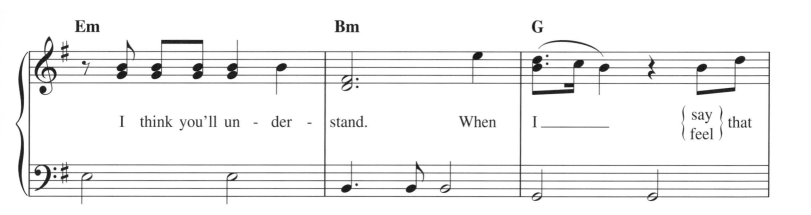

ONE OF US

Words and Music by
ERIC BAZILIAN

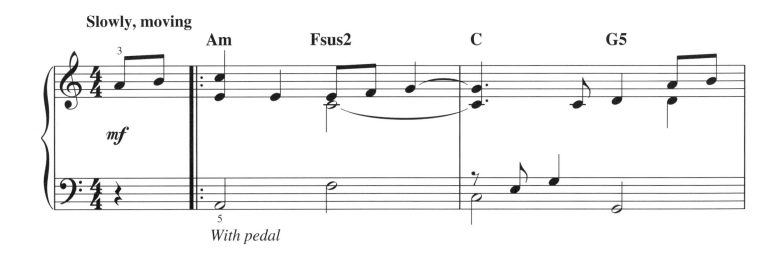

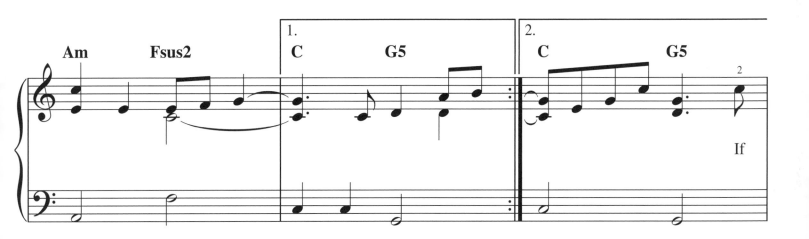

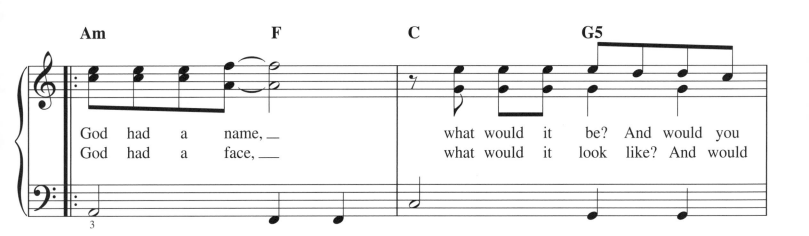

God had a name, ___
God had a face, ___

what would it be? And would you
what would it look like? And would

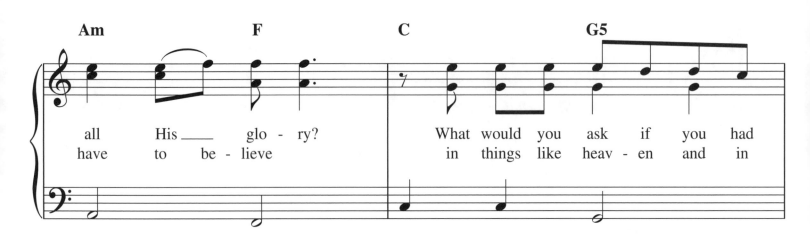

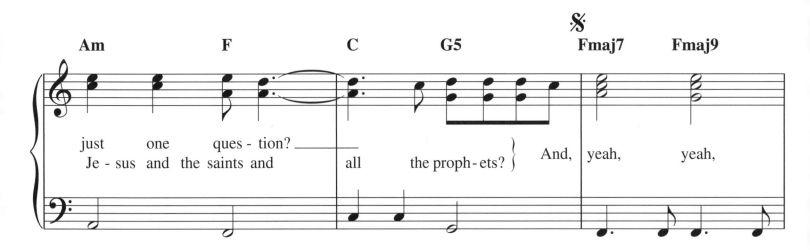

Yeah,   yeah,   yeah, yeah, yeah. What if God was one of us,

just a slob like one of us,   just a

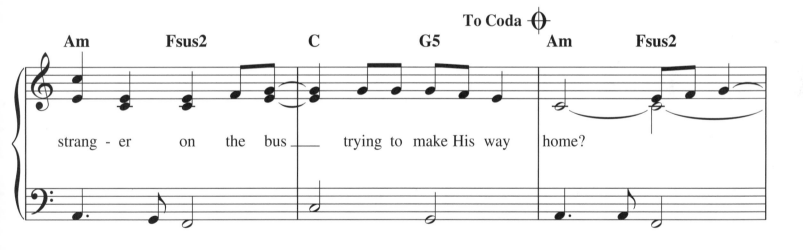

To Coda ⊕

strang - er   on   the   bus ___ trying to make His way   home?

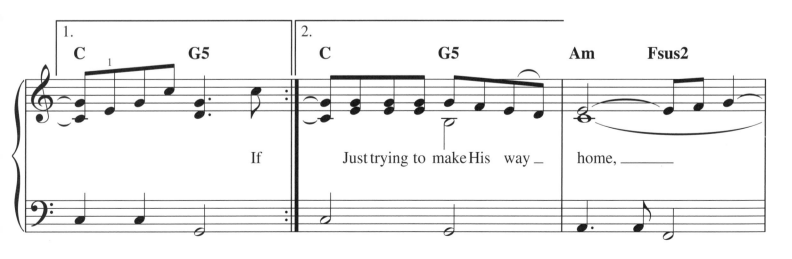

1.   2.

If   Just trying to make His way ___ home, ___

back up to heav-en all a - lone. _____ No-bod - y call-ing on the

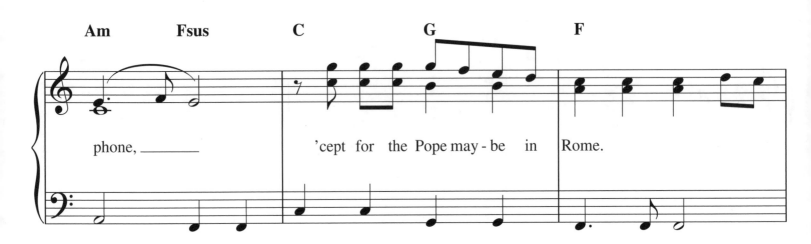

phone, _____ 'cept for the Pope may - be in Rome.

And,

home, just trying to make His way _ home, _____

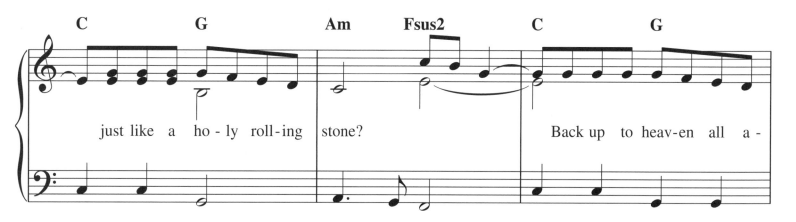

RIVER DEEP - MOUNTAIN HIGH

Words and Music by JEFF BARRY,
ELLIE GREENWICH and PHIL SPECTOR

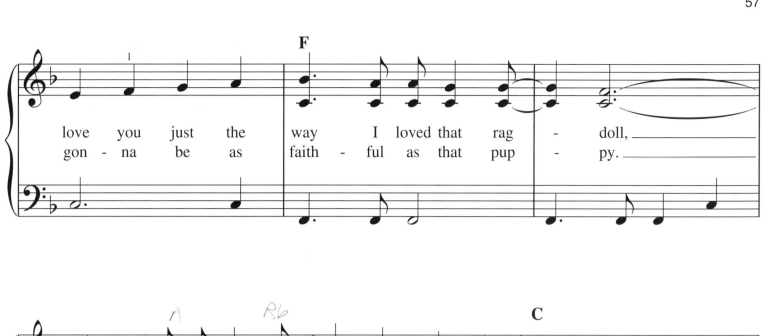

love you just the way I loved that rag - doll, _____
gon - na be as faith - ful as that pup - py. _____

_____ but on - ly now _____ my love has grown. _____
_____ You know I'll nev - er let you down. _____

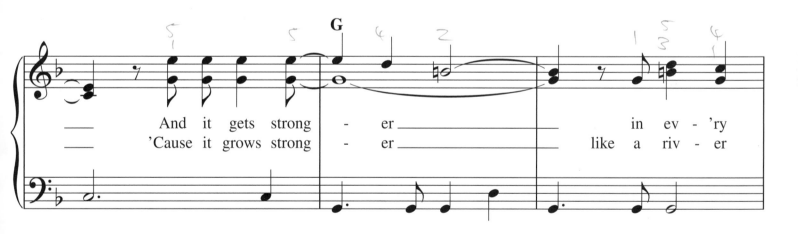

_____ And it gets strong - er _____ in ev - 'ry
_____ 'Cause it grows strong - er _____ like a riv - er

way, _____ and it gets deep - er,
flows, _____ and it gets big - ger,

let me say, _____ and it gets high-
and heav - en knows, _____ and it gets sweet-

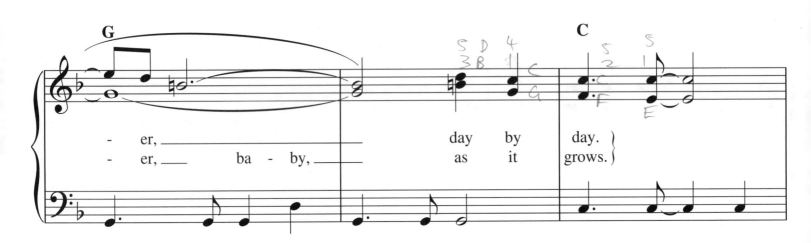

- er, _____ day by day.
- er, _____ ba - by, _____ as it grows.

Do I love _____ you, my oh my? _____

_____ Riv - er deep, _____

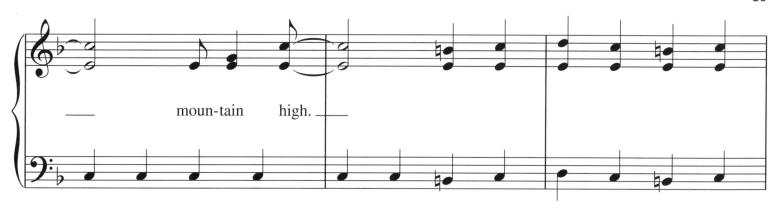

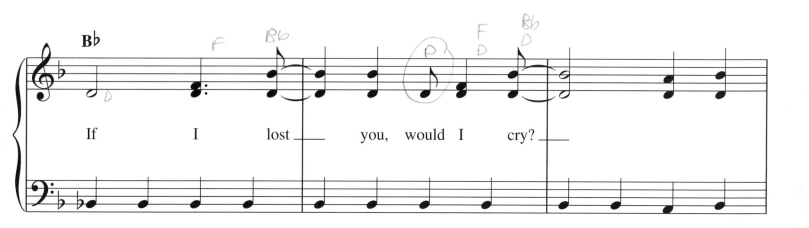

If I lost ___ you, would I cry? ___

Oh, how I love you, ba - by,

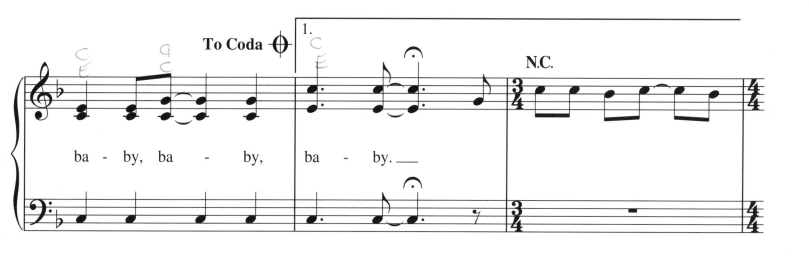

ba - by, ba - by, ba - by. ___

When you

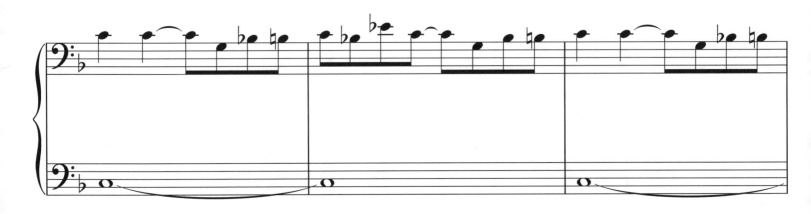

were a young boy, ba - by.

I love you, ba - by, like _ a

3

flow - er loves _ the spring; _____ and I love you, ba -

- by, like _ the rob - in loves _ to sing. _____

I love you, ba - by, like _ a school - boy loves his

pie; and I love you, ba - by, riv - er

deep   and moun - tain   high.

C

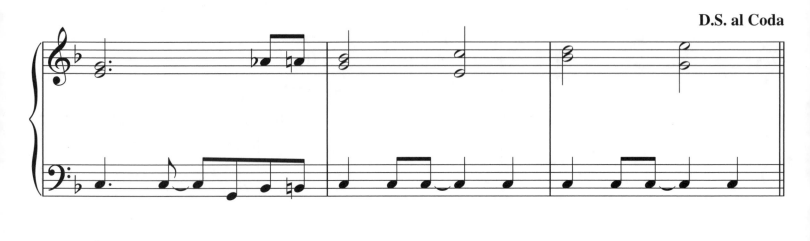

D.S. al Coda

CODA

ba - by. ____

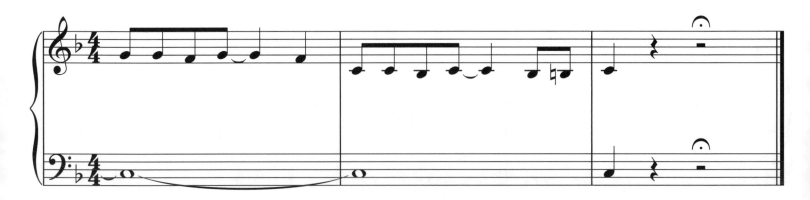

LUCKY

Words and Music by JASON MRAZ,
COLBIE CAILLAT and TIMOTHY FAGAN

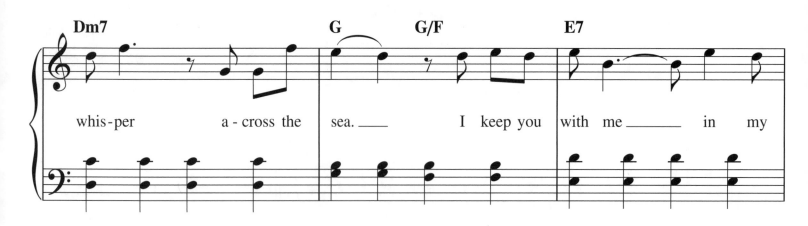

whis-per a - cross the sea.___ I keep you with me ___ in my

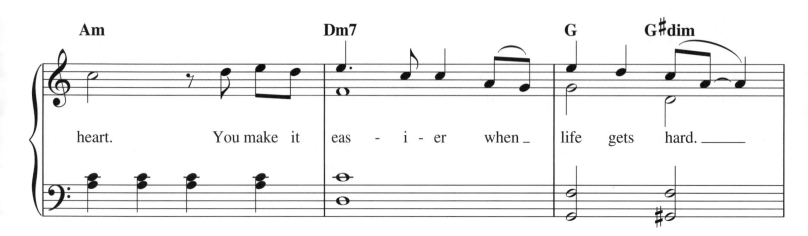

heart. You make it eas - i - er when _ life gets hard.___

Luck - y I'm in ___ love with my best friend, ___ luck - y to have _

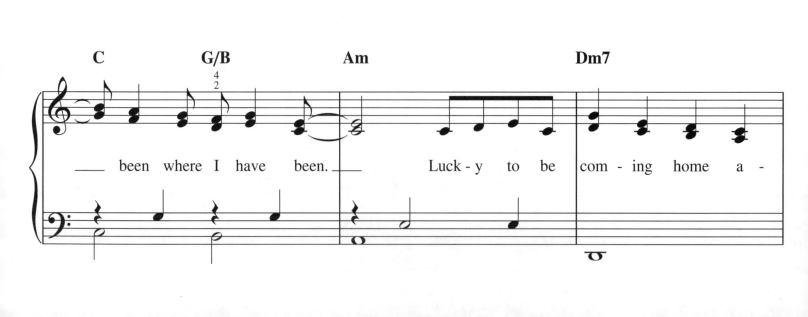

___ been where I have been. Luck - y to be com - ing home a -

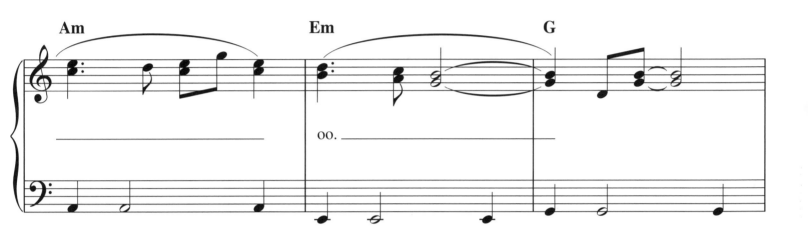

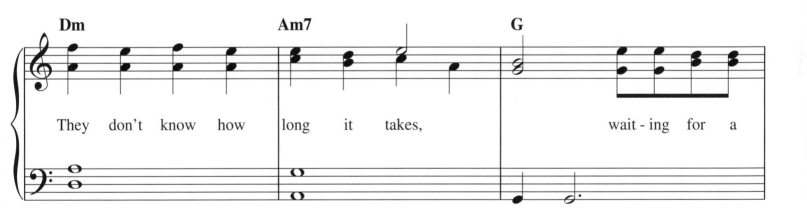

I wish we had one more kiss. I'll wait for you, I

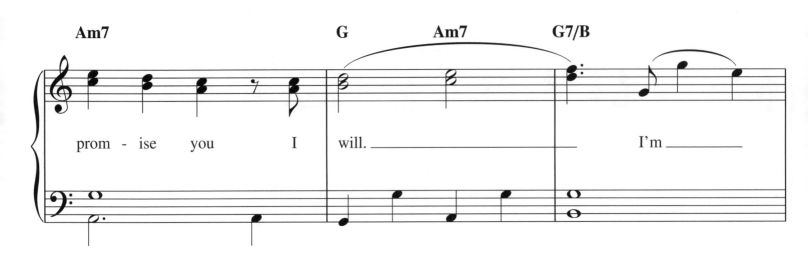

prom - ise you I will. _____ I'm _____

luck- y
Luck- y } I'm in ____ love with my best friend, ____ luck - y to have _

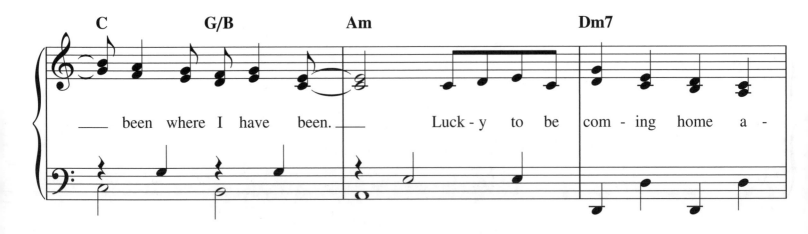

____ been where I have been. ____ Luck - y to be com - ing home a -

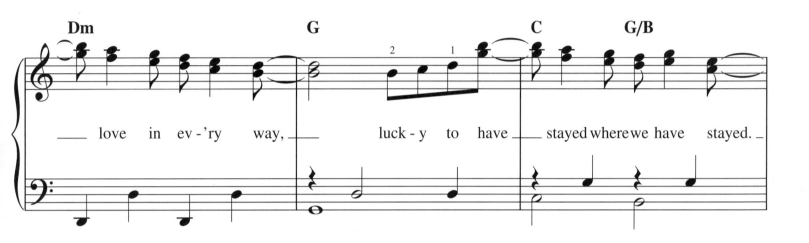

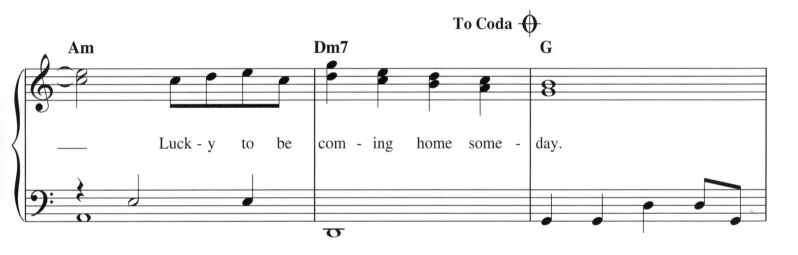

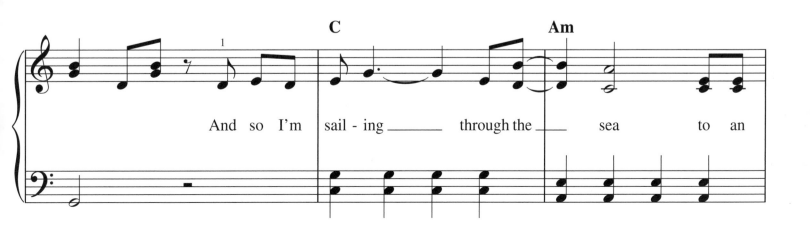

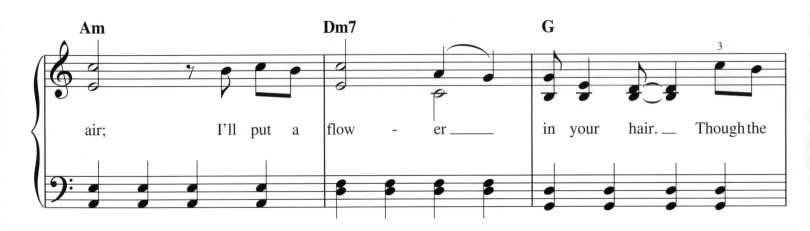

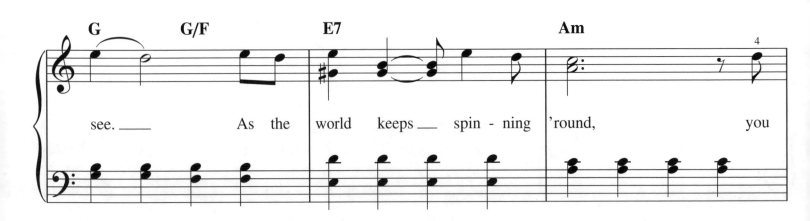

ONE LOVE

Words and Music by
BOB MARLEY

One love, one heart.

Let's   get   to - geth - er and   feel   all   right. { Hear the chil - dren
As it was in the be -
I'm plead - ing to ____

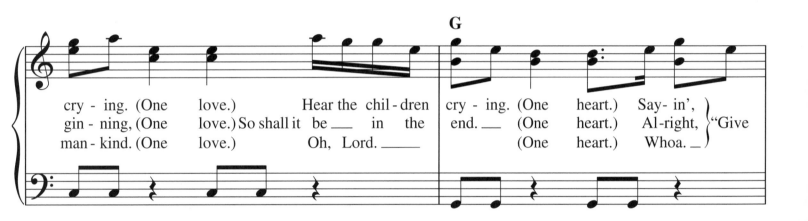

cry - ing. (One   love.)   Hear the chil - dren   cry - ing. (One   heart.) Say - in',
gin - ning, (One   love.) So shall it be ___ in the   end. ___ (One   heart.) Al - right, { "Give
man - kind. (One   love.)   Oh, Lord. _____   (One   heart.) Whoa. _

To Coda

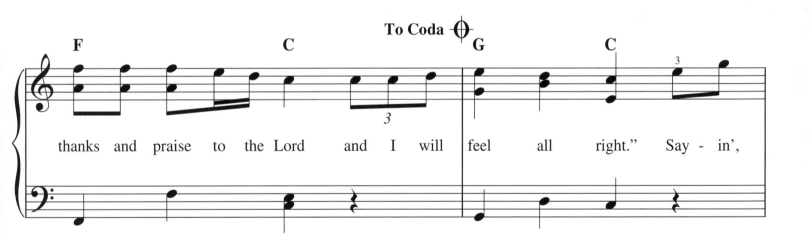

thanks and praise to the Lord   and I will   feel   all   right." Say - in',

"Let's   get   to - geth - er and   feel   all   right." { Whoa, whoa, whoa, whoa.
One   more ___ thing.

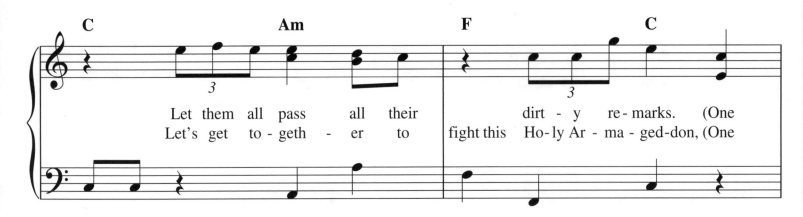

Let them all pass all their dirt - y re - marks. (One
Let's get to - geth – er to fight this Ho - ly Ar - ma - ged-don, (One

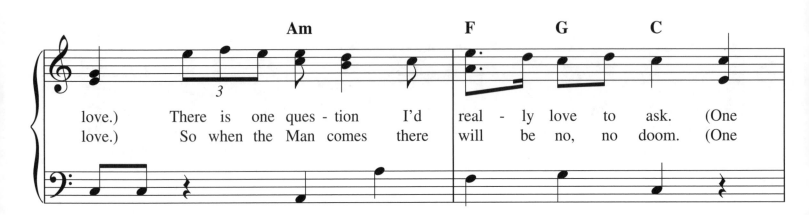

love.) There is one ques - tion I'd real - ly love to ask. (One
love.) So when the Man comes there will be no, no doom. (One

heart.) Is there a place __ for the hope - less sin - ner who has
song.) Have pit - y on those __ whose chanc - es grow thin - ner. There ain't

hurt all man-kind just to save his own? Be - lieve me.
no hid - ing place from the

TEENAGE DREAM

Words and Music by LUKASZ GOTTWALD,
MAX MARTIN, BENJAMIN LEVIN,
BONNIE McKEE and KATY PERRY

Moderate Dance beat

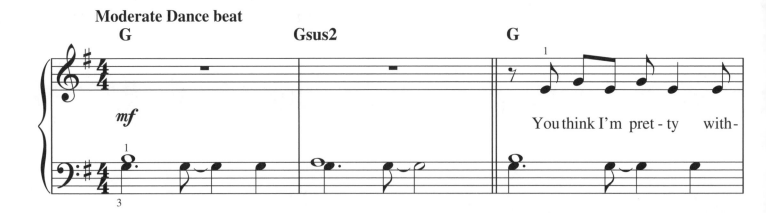

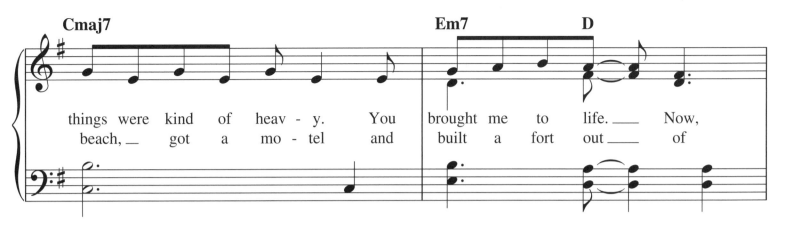

things were kind of heav - y. You
beach, _ got a mo - tel You and

brought me to life. _ Now,
built a fort out _ of

ev - 'ry Feb - ru - a - ry, _
sheets. I fi - n'lly found you, _

you'll be my val - en -
my miss - ing puz - zle

tine, _____ val - en - tine. ___ }
piece. ____ I'm com - plete. ___ }

Let's go all the way _

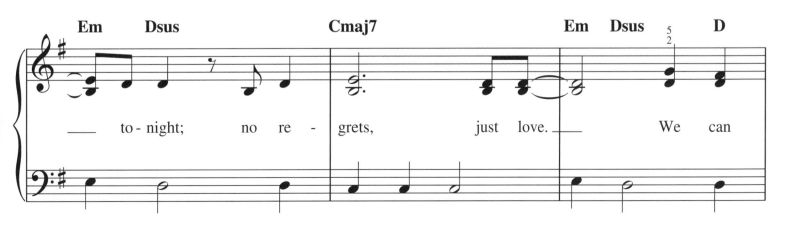

_ to - night; no re - grets, just love. _ We can

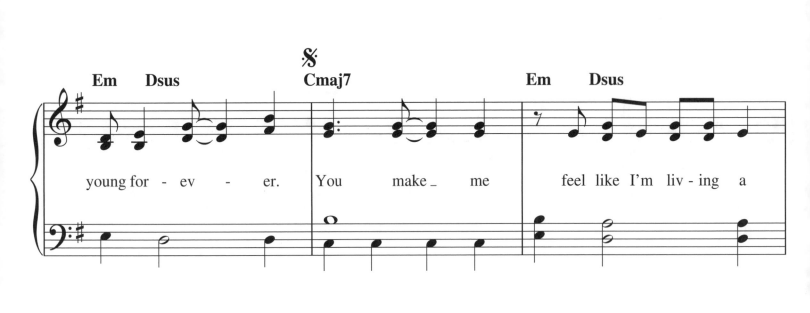

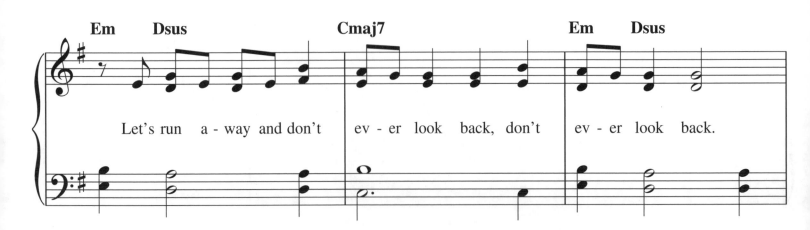

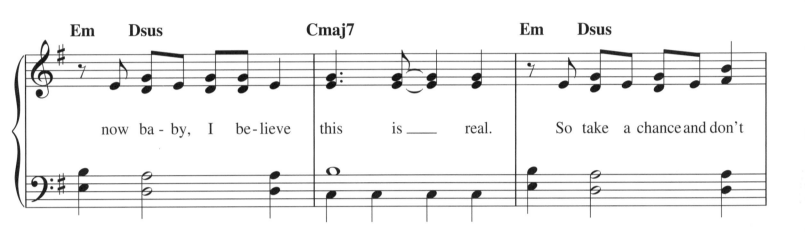

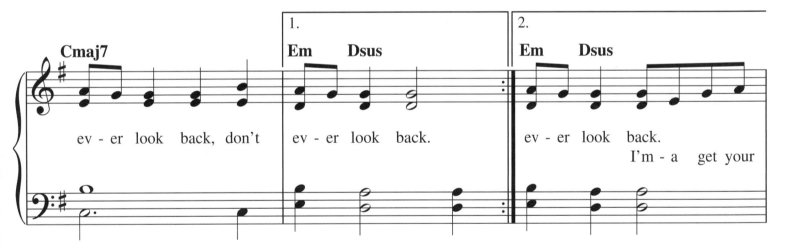

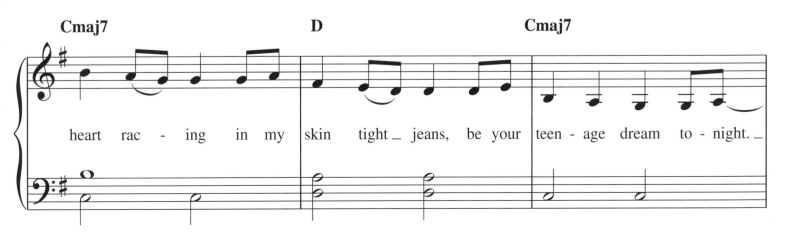

78

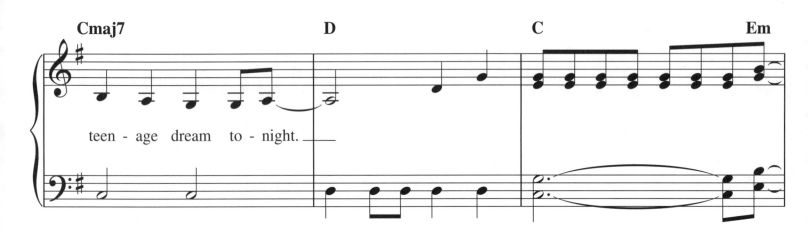

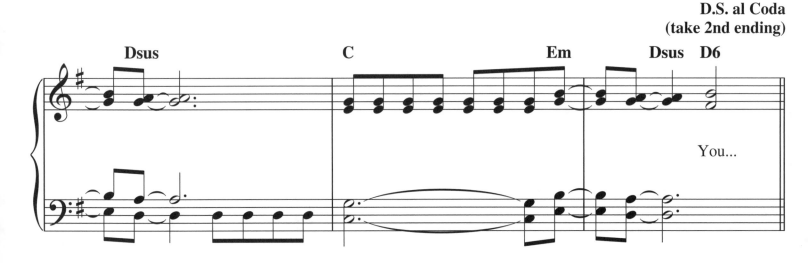

FORGET YOU

Words and Music by BRUNO MARS,
ARI LEVINE, PHILIP LAWRENCE,
THOMAS CALLAWAY and BRODY BROWN

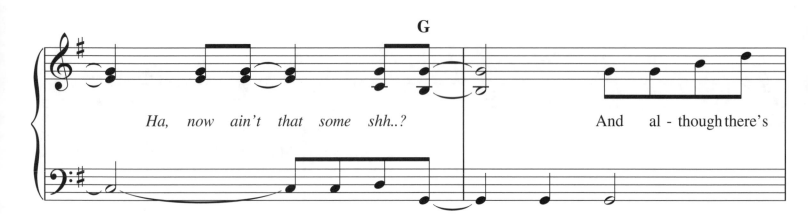

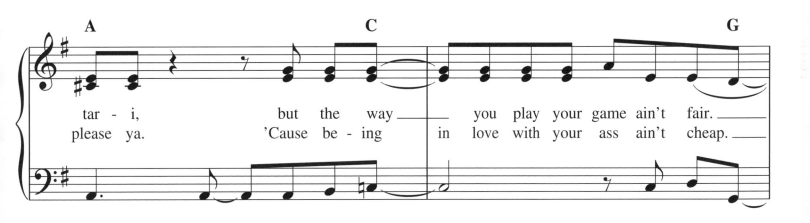

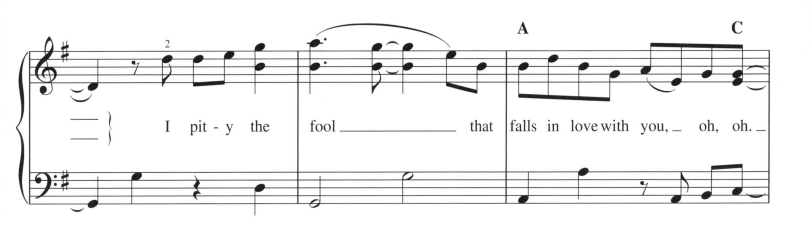

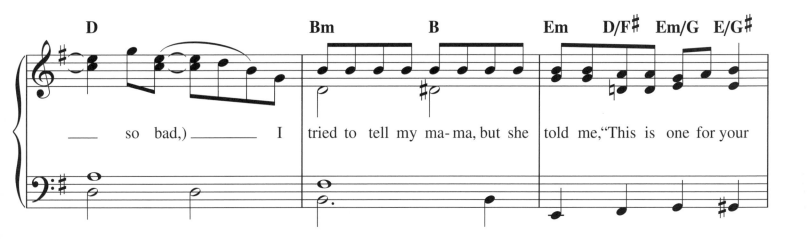

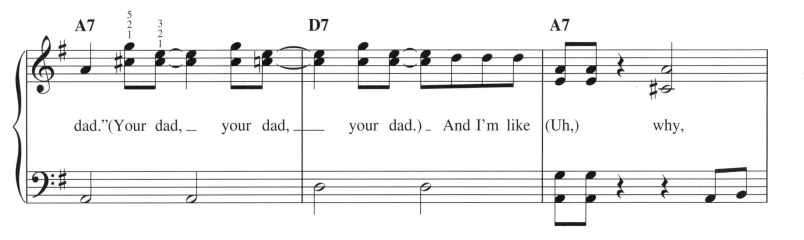

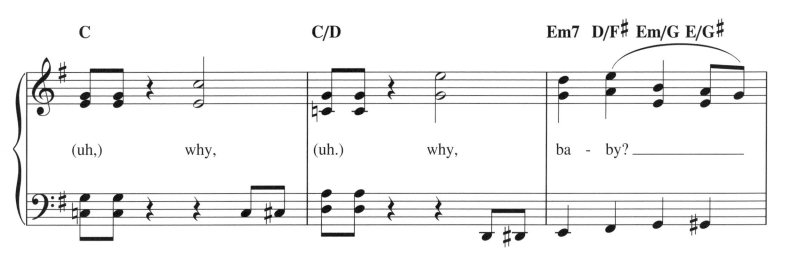

84

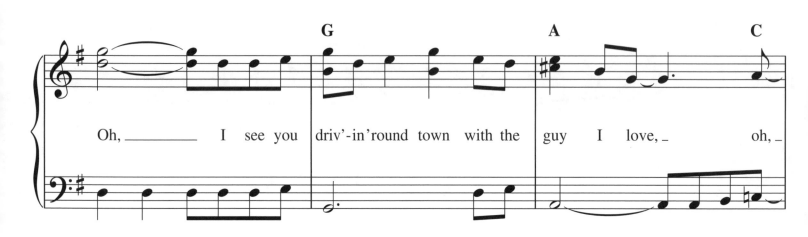

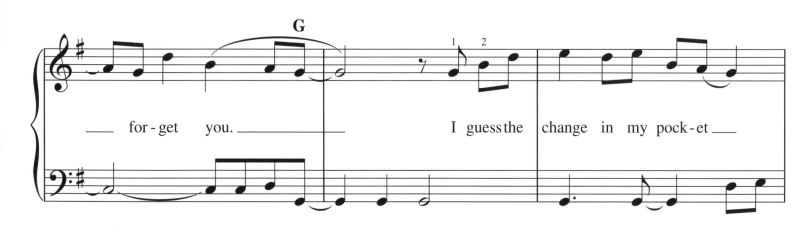

MARRY YOU

Words and Music by BRUNO MARS,
ARI LEVINE and PHILIP LAWRENCE

Moderately fast

It's a beau-ti-ful night.

We're look-ing for some-thing dumb to do. _____

_____ Hey, ba - by, _____ I think I wan-na mar-ry you. _

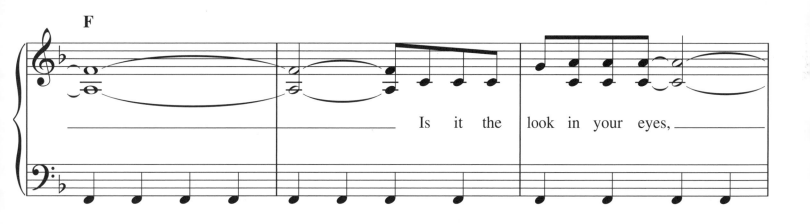

_____ Is it the look in your eyes, _____

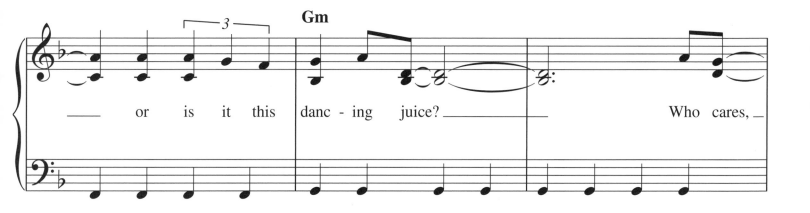

_____ or is it this danc-ing juice? _____ Who cares, _

baby; ___ I think I wan-na mar-ry you. ___

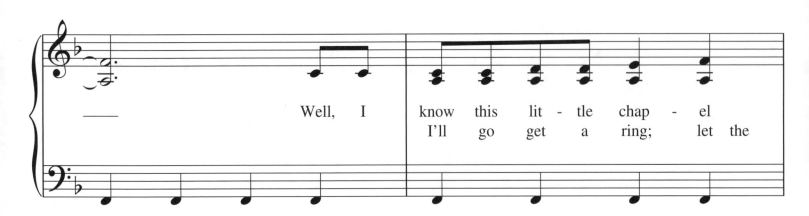

___ Well, I know this lit - tle chap - el
I'll go get a ring; let the

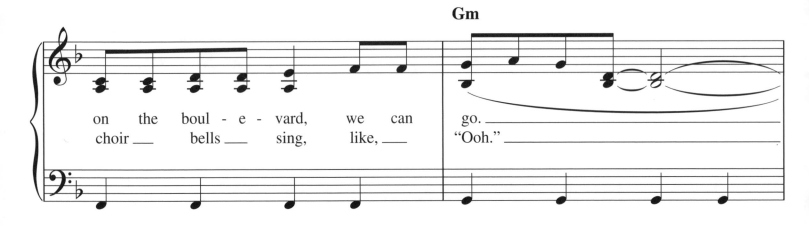

on the boul - e - vard, we can go. ___
choir ___ bells ___ sing, like, ___ "Ooh." ___

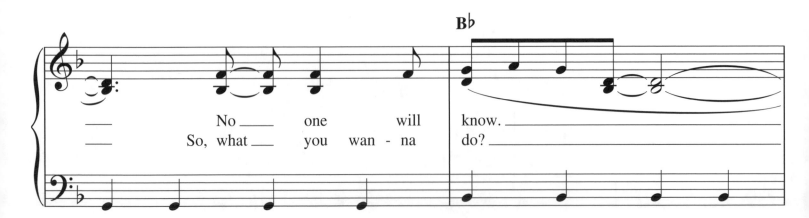

___ No ___ one will know. ___
___ So, what ___ you wan - na do? ___

Oh, come on, _____ girl. _____ Who
Let's just run, _____ girl. _____

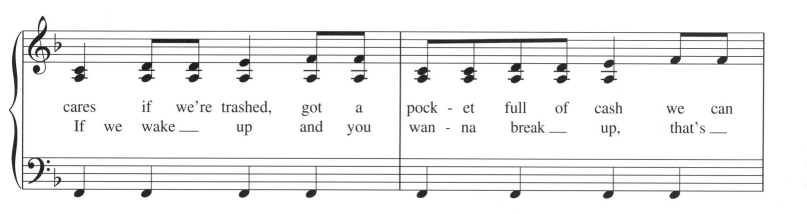

cares if we're trashed, got a pock - et full of cash we can
If we wake __ up and you wan - na break __ up, that's __

blow. _____ Shots __ of Pa - trón _____
cool. _____ No, I _____ won't blame you; _____

_____ and it's on, _____ girl. _____ Don't say
_____ it was fun, _____ girl. _____

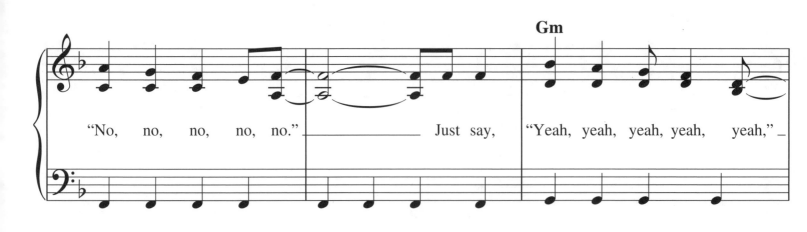

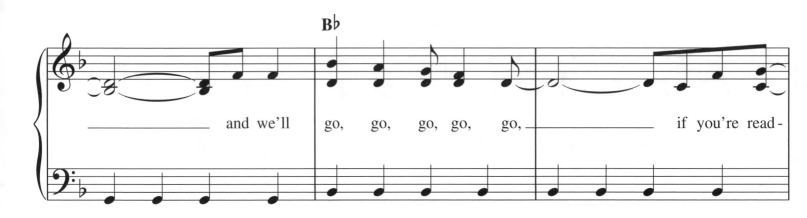

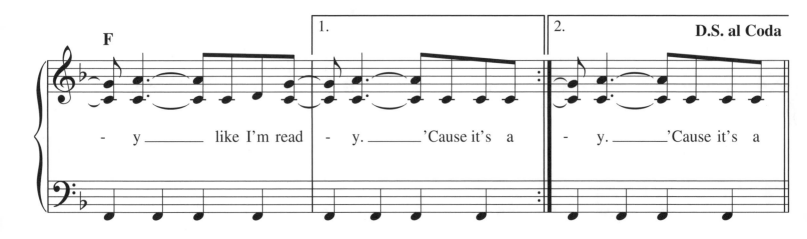

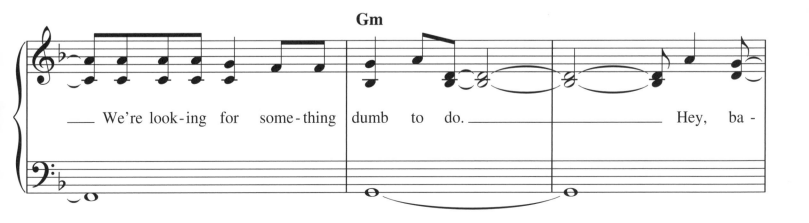

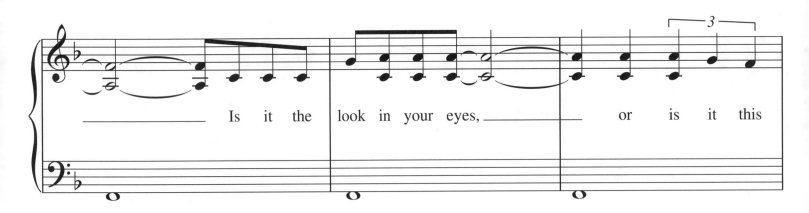

SWAY
(Quien Será)

English Words by NORMAN GIMBEL,
Spanish Words and Music by PABLO BELTRAN RUIZ

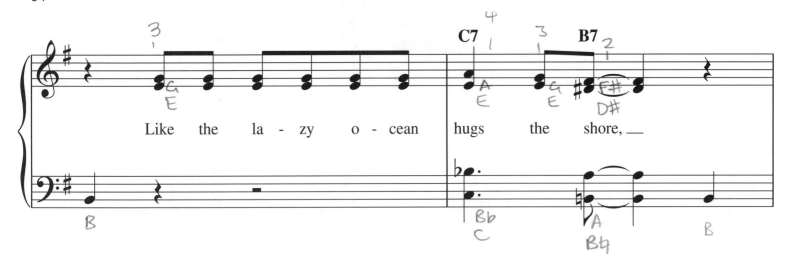

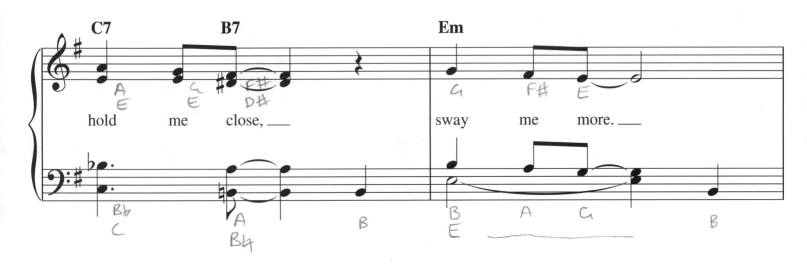

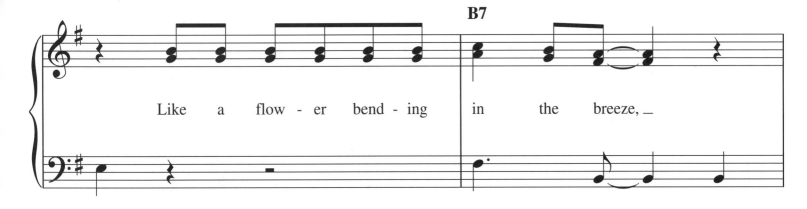

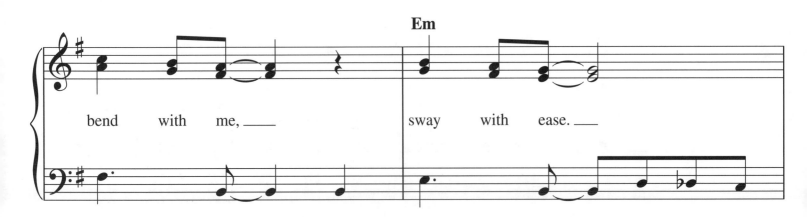

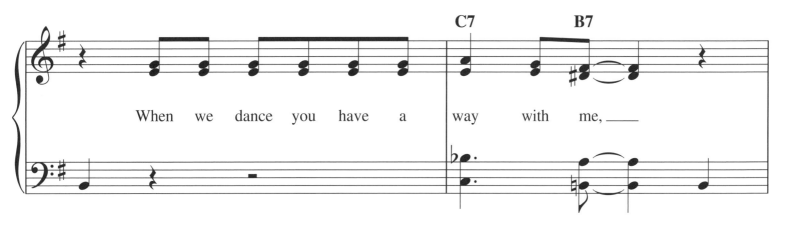

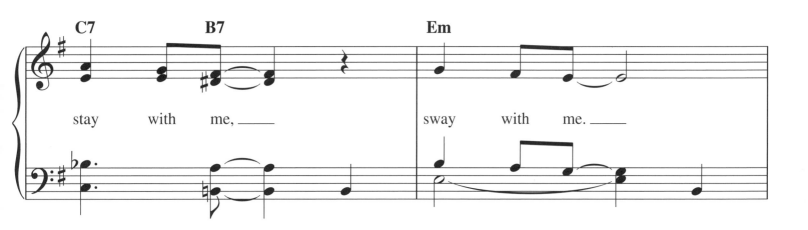

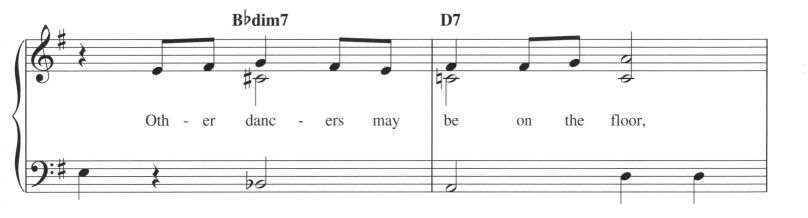

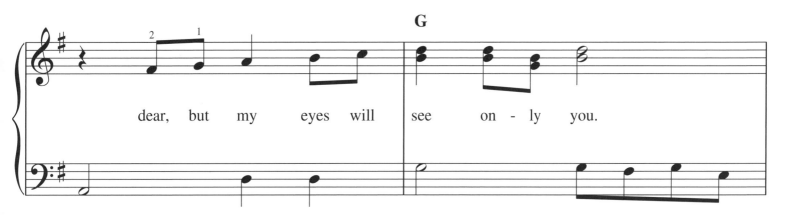

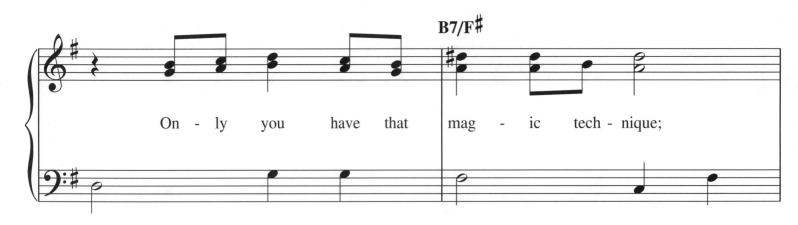

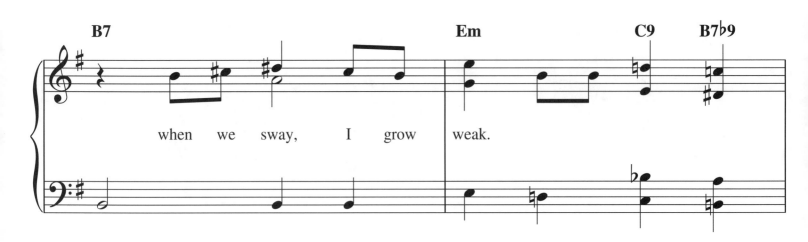

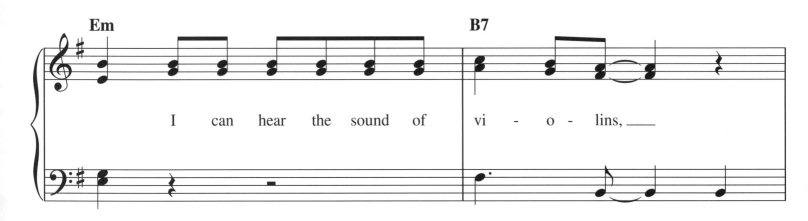

JUST THE WAY YOU ARE

Words and Music by BRUNO MARS,
ARI LEVINE, PHILIP LAWRENCE,
KHARI CAIN and KHALIL WALTON

Moderate Hip-Hop groove

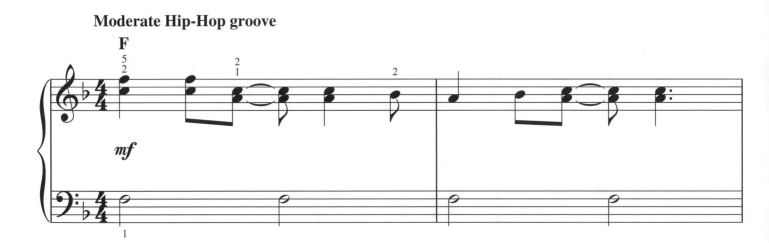

Oh, her eyes, __ her eyes __ make the stars look like they're not shin - in'.

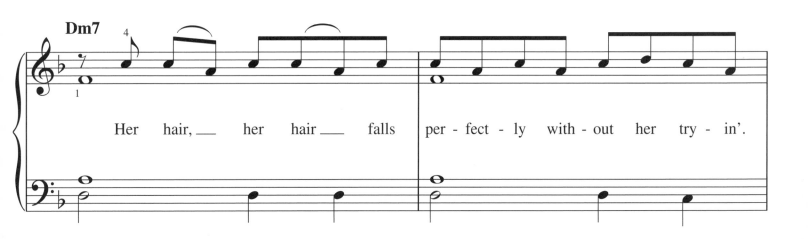

Dm7

Her hair, __ her hair __ falls per - fect - ly with - out her try - in'.

F/B♭   **F**

She's so beau - ti - ful, and I tell her ev - 'ry day.

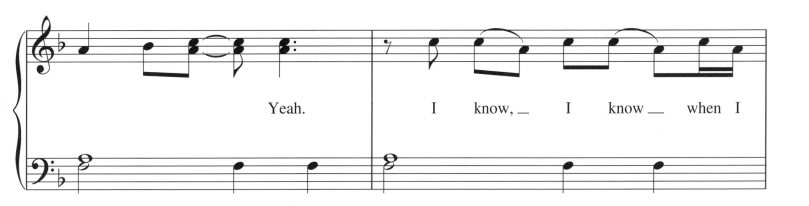

Yeah. I know, __ I know __ when I

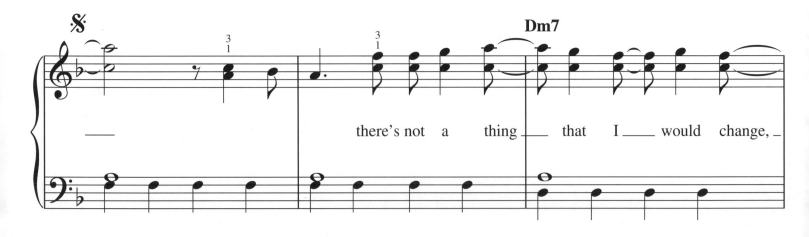

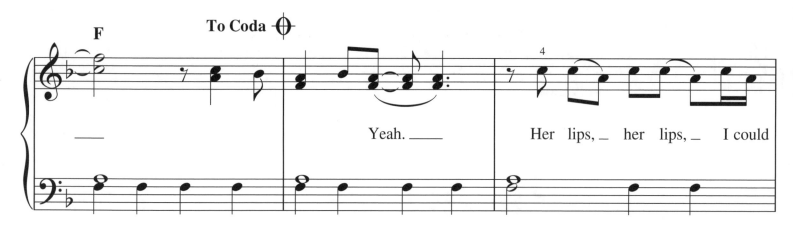

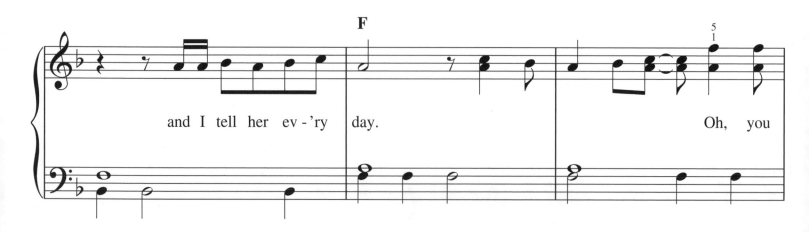

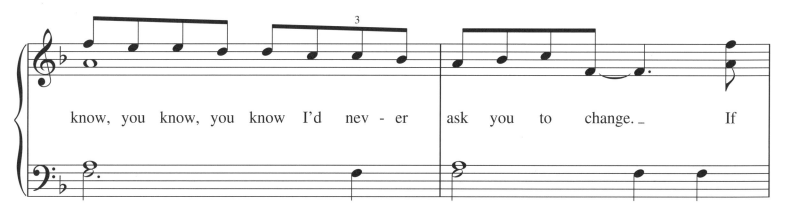

know, you know, you know I'd nev - er   ask   you   to   change. _   If

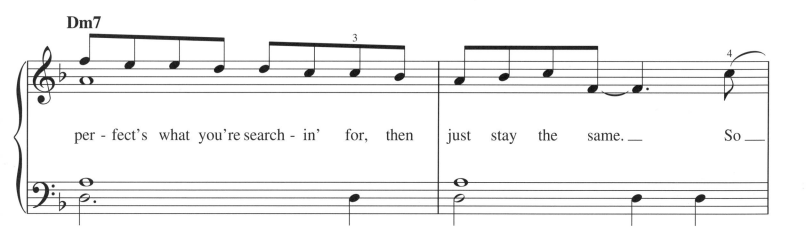

Dm7

per - fect's what you're search - in'   for, then   just   stay   the   same. _   So _

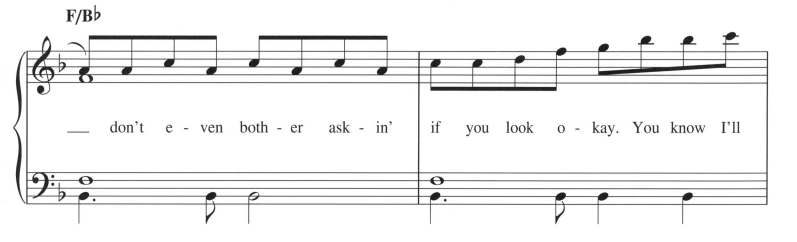

F/Bb

_ don't e - ven both - er ask - in'   if   you   look   o - kay. You know I'll

F

say: _____   When I see your face, _

D.S. al Coda

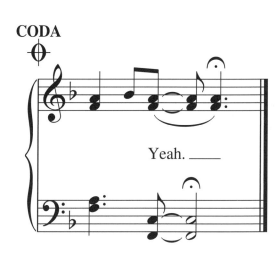

CODA

Yeah. ____

VALERIE

Words and Music by SEAN PAYNE,
DAVID McCABE, ABIGAIL HARDING,
BOYAN CHOWDHURY and RUSSELL PRITCHARD

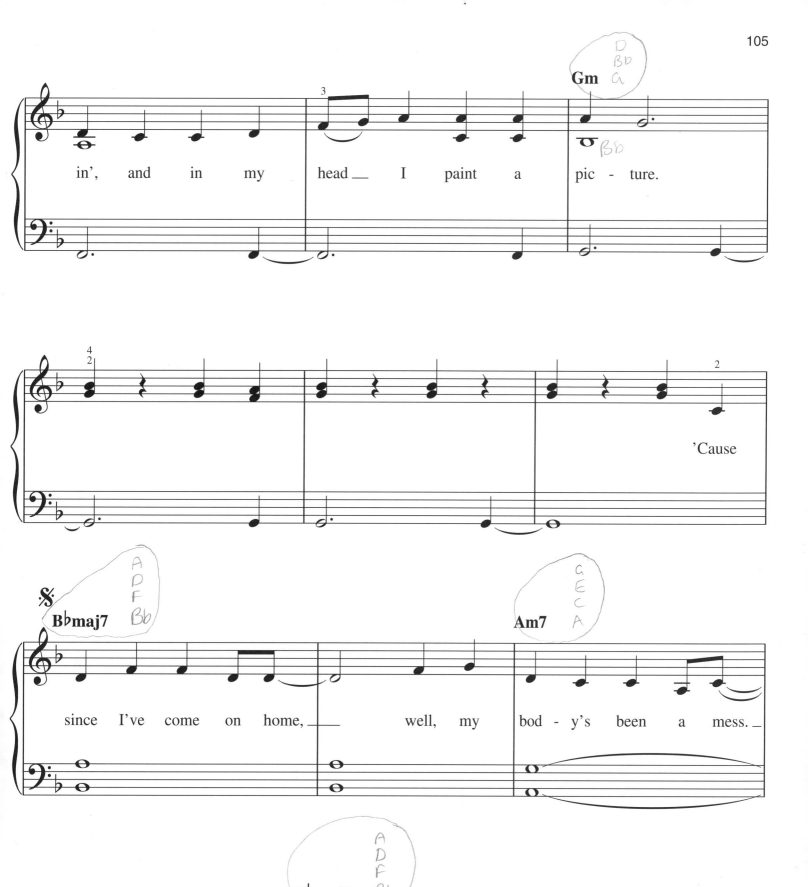

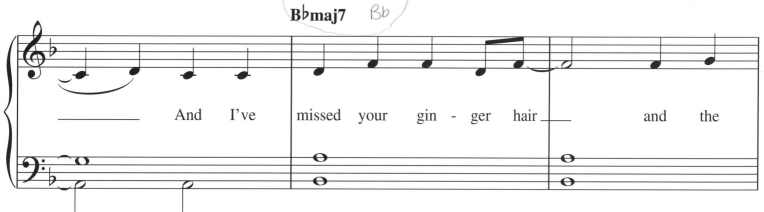

106

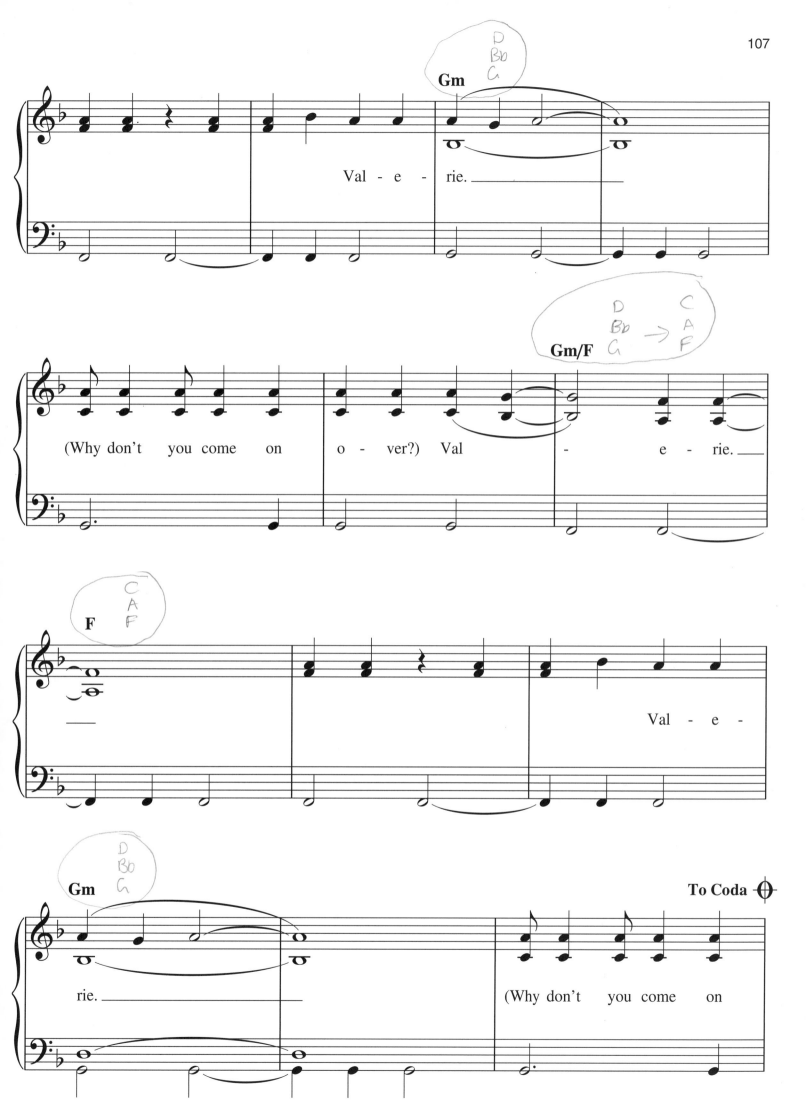

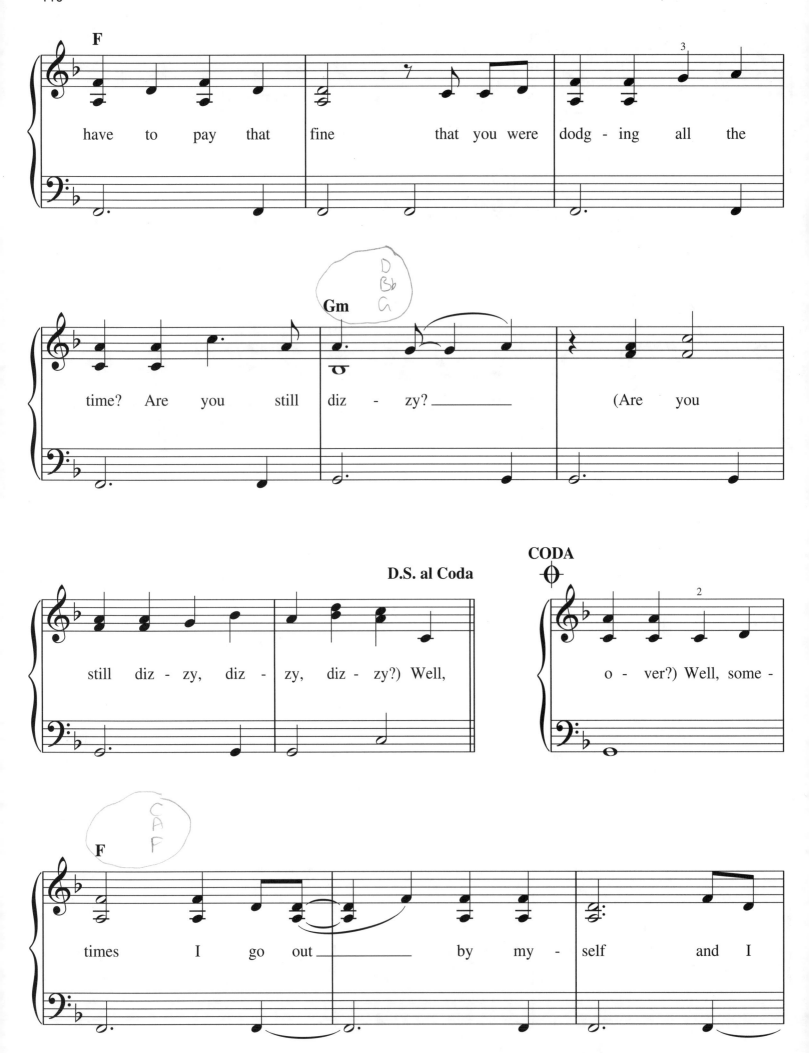

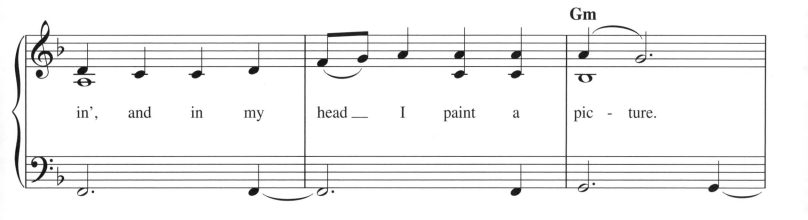

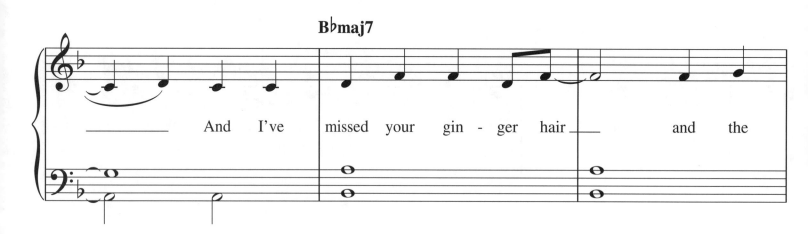

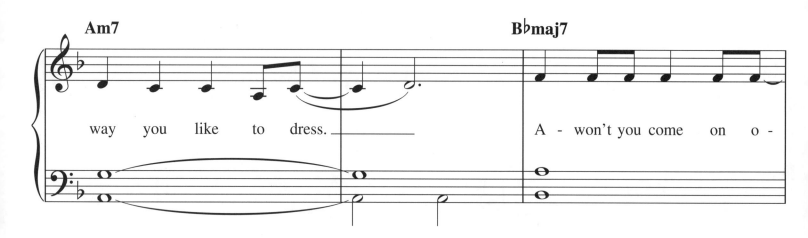

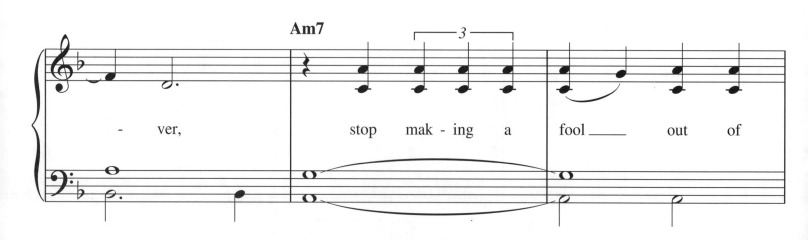

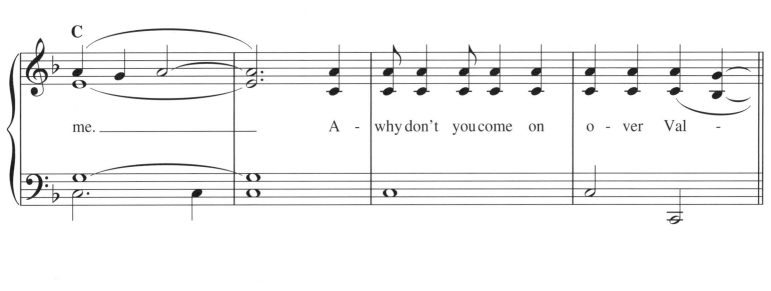

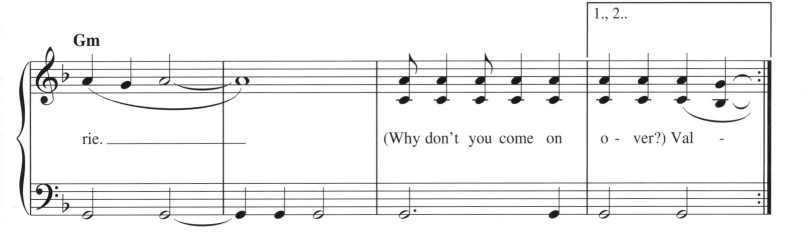

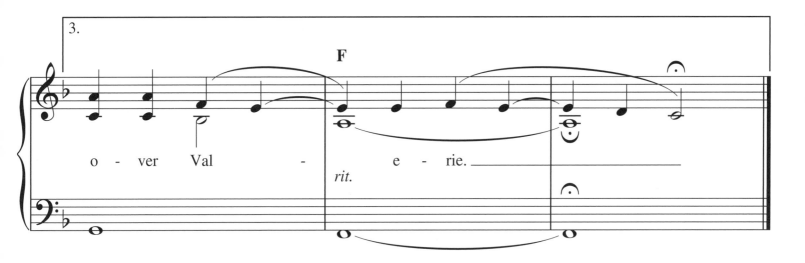

(I've Had)
THE TIME OF MY LIFE

Words and Music by FRANKE PREVITE,
JOHN DeNICOLA and DONALD MARKOWITZ

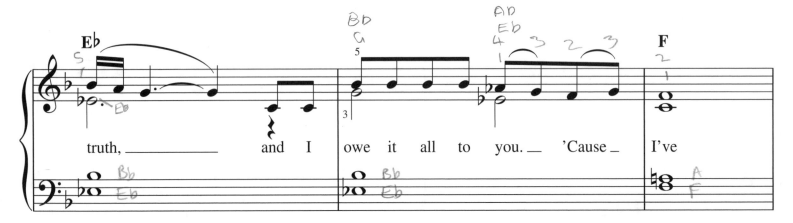

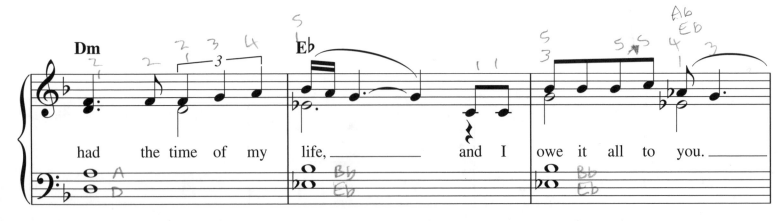

pas - sion in our eyes there's no way we could dis - guise it se - cret -

ly. _____ So we take each oth-er's hand 'cause we

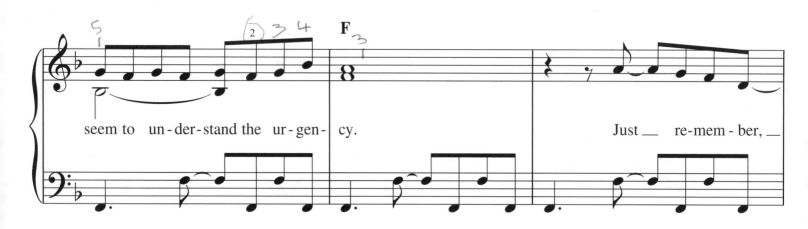

seem to un - der - stand the ur - gen - cy. Just __ re - mem - ber, __

__ you're the one thing I can't get e - nough __ of. _____

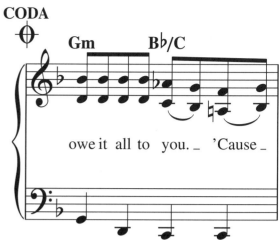

night. _   Stay with me.   Just re-mem-ber, _   owe it all to you. _   'Cause _

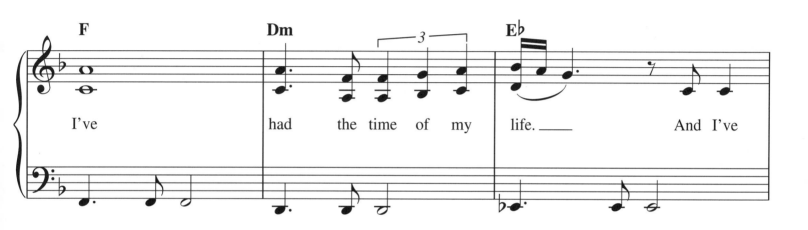

I've   had   the time of my   life. _____   And I've

searched through ev-'ry o-pen door   till I   found   the _ truth, _

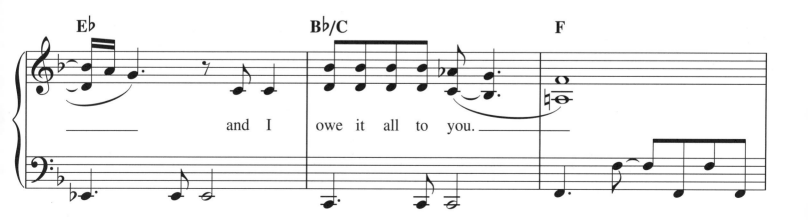

_____   and I   owe it all to you. _____

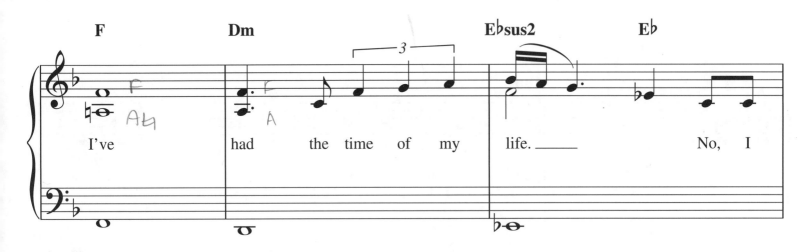

I've had the time of my life. _____ No, I

nev - er felt ___ this way be - fore. Yes, I swear it's the

truth ___ and I owe it all to you. ___